THE ELEMENTS OF
SOCIAL SCIENTIFIC
THINKING

THE ELEMENTS OF SOCIAL SCIENTIFIC THINKING Sixth Edition

Kenneth Hoover
Western Washington University

Todd Donovan
Western Washington University

St. Martin's Press   New York

Editor: Sabra Scribner
Managing editor: Patricia Mansfield Phelan
Project editor: Talvi Laev
Production supervisor: Joe Ford
Art director: Sheree Goodman
Cover design: Ruth Kolbert
Cover art: Laszló Mohony-Nagy, Composition A XXI (1925),
       Westfälisches Landesmuseum für Kunst und
       Kulturgeschichte Münster, R. Wakonigg

Library of Congress Catalog Card Number: 94–65240

9 8 7 6 5
f e d c b a

For information, write to:
St. Martin's Press, Inc.
175 Fifth Avenue
New York, NY 10010

ISBN: 0–312–09643–7

To our families

PREFACE

This little book is not very complicated. It is, rather, an initiation into social science intended for those who use the results of social science research and for those taking their first steps as researchers. Where do concepts come from? What is a variable? Why bother with scientific thinking? How is a hypothesis different from other statements about reality? How is it similar? These and other fundamental questions are dealt with here.

Our intent has been to help readers see through some false images of social science and to say enough to make the first steps in research possible for them, while leaving to more detailed and specialized sources the elaboration of the technicalities of research operations. Throughout, the emphasis is on reality testing as a process by which we can know what to make of the world. This presentation of science is not a narrow one—we encourage the reader to be scientific in daily thought as well as in the specific application of social scientific methods.

Changes in the Sixth Edition

After twenty years of experience with five editions of this text, the time seemed right for a major updating and revision to take account of contemporary needs. The partnership formed with this edition combines the perspectives of a political theorist, Kenneth Hoover, and a behavioral analyst, Todd Donovan. Although we have not changed the emphasis on straightforward explanation, we have expanded the discussion of topics such as validity, reliability, and regression; chosen new examples; and improved the references. New appendixes were selected to serve as illustrations of social scientific thinking, and this has meant considerable revision of chapters Four and Five. Questions for discussion have been added at the end of the first five chapters. We hope you will find that our joint approach makes for richer understanding and better communication.

Our conviction is that the debate between social scientists who quantify and those who don't (and between positivists and anti-positivists) has served the valuable purpose of broadening the array of tools and perspectives available to social scientists. This debate has also absorbed a huge amount of energy and enterprise that would now be better directed at making constructive use of all the techniques of social analysis. If nothing else, it is evident that no one approach holds all the answers, and that every approach has its particular pitfalls and openings to prejudice. Choosing the appropriate methodology, or combination of methodologies, is the critical consideration.

While social scientists have been occupied with these debates, society's problems seem to have grown more complex and difficult to resolve. If careful observation is critical in understanding these problems, then social science has a key role to play. The classic rules of scientific inquiry provide a framework for resolving conflicts over that most contentious matter, the truth, even between people who don't particularly like each other. Useful ideas from all sources of insight badly need to be tested through systematic analysis so that conflicting points of view can be resolved into productive forms of action.

How to Read This Book

Most books are meant to be read straight through. For many readers, that will be the best approach for this book. However, the reader should be aware that each chapter surveys social scientific thinking at a different level. For that reason, there can be various points of access to the book depending on the reader's needs. The first chapter, "Thinking Scientifically," sets social science in the general context of the ways in which people try to answer questions about the world around them. Chapter Two, "The Elements of Science," develops the basic outline of the scientific method by discussing concepts, variables, measurements, hypotheses, and theory.

For those faced with the immediate task of doing or understanding research, Chapter Three, entitled "Strategies," may be a good place to begin because it deals directly with the nuts and bolts of scientific inquiry. Chapter Four, "Refinements," presumes a basic understanding of the scientific method explained in Chapter Two and provides additional research tools. Chapter Five is devoted to the art and science of measurement. Chapter Six, "Reflections: Back to the Roots," should be read, we think, by those who use the book for any purpose. The point of this concluding chapter is to place scientific understanding in perspective and to suggest generally where humility is advisable and achievement possible.

For convenience of access and review, each chapter begins with an outline of the topics covered and ends with a list of the major concepts introduced, in their order of appearance.

In Appendix A, an article entitled "Schematic Assessments of Presidential Candidates" by Arthur Miller, Martin Wattenberg, and Oksana Malanchuk is reprinted in condensed form. The article is cited frequently in the text; those who need a good model for the design and analysis of a research topic will want to consider it carefully. Appendix B consists of an article entitled "Do Black Judges Make a Difference?" by Susan Welch, Michael Combs, and John Gruhl. Appendix B is relevant only to the section on regression analysis in Chapter Five.

We invite readers of *The Elements of Social Scientific Thinking* to share their assessments with us. We can be reached at the Department of Political Science, Western Washington University, Bellingham, WA 98225, or we can be contacted by e-mail at Khoover @henson.cc.wwu.edu or donovan@nessie.cc.wwu.edu.

Acknowledgments

The numerous critics and commentators who have contributed to the refinement of this book over the years are now too many to list. Readers should be aware that the insights of a great many friends, teachers, and students are found in these pages. Bob Blair of the College of Wooster Sociology Department was a good friend and trusty resource as the first edition was being written. We are grateful to one wise and perceptive critic who has been with this book since its first edition, Aage Clausen of Ohio State University. Shaun Bowler of the University of California—Riverside offered useful suggestions for this edition. In addition, we would like to make special mention of colleagues at Western Washington University whose interest and suggestions on methodology have been most useful: Dana Jack, John Richardson, Carl Simpson, and Sara Weir.

Working with Louise Waller, Sabra Scribner, and their colleagues at St. Martin's Press has been a considerable pleasure. To all of these we are indeed indebted, as are the readers of this book, though neither they nor we may hold them responsible for the result.

Judy Hoover contributed some helpful suggestions in the writing, and a great deal more besides. Andrew and Erin Hoover appear briefly in the second chapter and are present throughout in the nurture of the spirit they provide to their father.

Kenneth Hoover
Western Washington University

Todd Donovan
Western Washington University

CONTENTS

Contents

THE ELEMENTS OF
SOCIAL SCIENTIFIC
THINKING

OUTLINE

CHAPTER ONE

THINKING SCIENTIFICALLY

"Science searches the common experience of people; and it is made by people, and it has their style."

JACOB BRONOWSKI

"Social science" in cold print gives rise to images of some robot in a statistics laboratory reducing human activity to bloodless digits and simplified formulas. Research reports filled with mechanical-sounding words such as "empirical," "quantitative," "operational," "inverse," and "correlative" aren't very poetic. Yet the stereotypes of social science created by these images are, we will try to show, wrong.

Like any other mode of knowing, social science can be used for perverse ends; however, it can also be used for humane personal understanding. By testing thoughts against reality, science helps liberate inquiry from bias, prejudice, and just plain muddleheadedness. So it is unwise to be put off by simple stereotypes—too many people accept these stereotypes and deny themselves the power of social scientific understanding.

The word "science" stands for a very great deal in our

3

culture—some even consider it the successor to religion in the modern age. Our objective here is not to examine the whole tangle of issues associated with science; it is to find a path into the scientific way of thinking about things. In order to find that path, we will begin by allowing some descriptions of science to emerge out of contrasts with other forms of knowledge.

First, we have to identify some distractions that should be ignored. Science is sometimes confused with technology, which is the application of science to various tasks. Grade-school texts that caption pictures of voyages to the planets with the title "Science Marches On!" aid such confusion. The technology that makes such voyages possible emerged from the use of scientific strategies in the study of propulsion, electronics, and numerous other fields. It is the mode of inquiry that is scientific; the spacecraft is a piece of technology.

Just as science is not technology, neither is it some specific body of knowledge. The popular phrase "*Science tells us* [for example] that smoking can kill you" really misleads. "Science" doesn't tell us anything; people tell us things, in this case people who have used scientific strategies to investigate the relationship of smoking to cancer. Science, as a way of thought and investigation, is best conceived of as existing not in books, or in machinery, or in reports containing numbers, but rather in that invisible world of the mind. Science has to do with the way questions are formulated and answered; it is a set of rules and forms for inquiry created by people who want reliable answers.

Another distraction comes from identifying particular persons as "scientists." That usage isn't false, since the people so labeled practice the scientific form of inquiry; but neither is it fully honest to say that some people are scientists, whereas others are nonscientists. Some people specialize in scientific approaches to knowledge, but we are all participants in the scientific way of thinking. *Science is a mode of inquiry that is common to all human beings.*

In becoming more self-conscious of your own habits of

thought, you will find that there is a bit of the scientist in all of us. We measure, compare, modify beliefs, and acquire a kind of savvy about evidence in the daily business of figuring out what to do next and how to relate to others. The simplest of games involves the testing of tactics and strategies against the data of performance, and that is crudely scientific. Even trying out different styles of dress for their impact on others has an element of science in it.

The scientific way of thought is one of a number of strategies by which we try to cope with a vital reality: the uncertainty of life. We don't know what the consequences of many of our actions will be. We may have little idea of the forces that affect us subtly or directly, gradually or suddenly. In trying to accomplish even the simplest task, such as figuring out what to eat, we do elementary calculations of what might taste good or what might be good for us. If there's enough uncertainty on that score, a little advance testing is a good idea: the queen has her taster, and the rest of us, at least when it comes to a certain hamburger, have the assurance that billions have already been sold.

Science is *a process of thinking and asking questions,* not a body of knowledge. It is one of several ways of claiming that we know something. In one sense, the scientific method is a set of criteria for deciding how conflict about differing views of reality can be resolved. It offers a strategy that researchers can use when approaching a question. It offers "consumers" of research the ability to critically assess how evidence has been developed and used in reaching a conclusion.

The scientific approach has many competitors in the search for understanding. For many people throughout most of history, the competitors have prevailed. Analysis of reality has usually been much less popular than myths, superstitions, and hunches, which have the reassuring feel of certainty *before* the event they try to predict or control, though seldom afterwards. Sometimes unverified belief sponsors an inspired action or sustains the doubtful until a better day. Certainly personal beliefs are a vital part of our lives. The point is that the refusal to analyze is crippling, and the skilled analyst is in a position of strength.

Why Bother to Be Systematic?

Most human communication takes place among small groups of persons who share a common language and much common experience and understanding of the world they live in. There is a ready-made arena for mutual agreement. Not so in a more complex social environment. Though families can transmit wisdom across generations by handing down stories and maxims, societies run into trouble. In its most cynical form, the question is, "Whose story is to be believed?" The need to understand what is happening around us and to share experiences with others makes systematic thought and inquiry essential.

Because society is interesting for the drama it contains, there is a tendency to dispense with systematic understanding and get on with the descriptions, stories, and personal judgments. Although these can be illuminating, they often have limited usefulness because highly subjective accounts of life form a poor basis for the development of common understanding and common action.

The intricate task of getting people to bridge the differences that arise from the singularity of their experience requires a disciplined approach to knowledge. *Knowledge is socially powerful only if it is knowledge that can be put to use.* Social knowledge, if it is to be useful, must be *communicable, valid,* and *compelling.*

In order to be communicable, knowledge must be expressed in clear form. And if the knowledge is intended to be used as a spur to action, it must be valid in light of the appropriate evidence and compelling in the way that it fits the question raised. A personal opinion such as "I think that capitalism exploits the poor" may influence your friends and even your relatives to think that there is some injustice in our society. But it probably won't make any waves with others. If, however, you can cite the evidence that "Despite all the wealth in our society, one quarter of all children under the age of six are living in poverty," a more compelling argument results, because you relate a judgment to a measurement of reality.[1] People who don't even like you but who favor some kind of fairness in wealth distribution might find such a statement a powerful cue to examine our economic system critically. Knowledge built on evidence, and captured in clear transmissible form, makes for power over the environment.

Accumulating knowledge so that past mistakes can be avoided has always intrigued civilized humanity. One can record the sayings of wise persons, and that does contribute greatly to cultural enrichment. Yet there is surely room for another kind of cumulative effort: the building up of statements evidenced in a manner that can be double-checked by others. To double-check a statement requires that one know precisely what was claimed and how the claim was tested. This is a major part of the enterprise of science. The steps to be discussed in Chapter Two in the section on the scientific method are the guideposts for accomplishing that kind of knowing.

The Role of Reasoned Judgment and Opinion

All this vaguely ominous talk about systematic thinking is not meant to cast out reasoned judgment, opinion, and imagination. After all, there is no particular sense in limiting the facilities of the mind in any inquiry.

[1]See "Poverty in the U.S. Grew Faster Than Population in Last Year," *New York Times*, October 5, 1993, p. A10.

Reasoned judgment is a staple of human understanding. A reasoned judgment bears a respectable relationship to evidence. Because people inevitably have to act in the absence of complete evidence for decision making, the term "judgment" is important. Judgment connotes decision making in which all the powers of the mind are activated to make the best use of available knowledge.

Social science does not eliminate the role of judgment from the research process. Indeed, judgment plays a crucial role in how scientific evidence is gathered and evaluated. It is one thing to observe that the top 1 percent of our country's population control more wealth (not income) than the bottom 90 percent. It is another matter, however, to link this evidence to broad social questions about capitalism, poverty, wealth, exploitation, productivity, economic development, and other issues. Logic and good judgment are required to interpret the evidence.[2]

Reasoned judgment is the first part of systematic thought. The proposition that "A full moon on the eve of election day promotes liberal voting" could be correct, but it does not reflect much reasoned judgment, since there is neither evidence for linking the two events nor a logical connection between them. An investigator with time and resources might look into such a proposition, but in a world of scarce time, inadequate resources, and serious problems of social analysis to engage rare talents, such an investigation makes little sense.[3] Although the proposition may be intuitive, even intuition usually bears some relationship to experience and evidence.

Opinion likewise plays an inescapable role in scientific analysis, because all efforts at inquiry proceed from some per-

---

[2]See Sylvia Nasar, "Fed Report Gives New Data on Gains by Richest in 80's," *New York Times*, April 21, 1992, p. A1.

[3]However, police and bartenders will tell you that the night of a full moon does in fact bring out some pretty bizarre behavior; the hypothesis isn't completely preposterous.

sonal interest or other. No one asks a question unless there is an interest in what the conclusion might be. Furthermore, each person's angle of vision on reality is necessarily slightly different from the angle of another. Opinion can't be eliminated from inquiry, but it can be controlled so that it does not fly off into complete fantasy. One practice that assists in reducing the role of opinion is for the researcher to be conscious of his or her values and opinions.

Plato's famous aphorism, "Know thyself," applies here more than ever. Much damage has been done to the cause of good social science by those who pretend disinterest to the point at which their research conceals opinions that covertly structure their conclusions. No one is truly objective, certainly not about the nature of society—there are too many personal stakes involved for that.

Ultimately, good science provides its own check on the influence of values in an inquiry. If the method by which the study has been done and the evidence for conclusions are clearly and fully stated, the study can be examined for the fit of conclusions to evidence. If there is doubt about the validity of what has been done, the study itself can be double-checked, or "replicated," to use the technical term. This feature distinguishes science from personal judgment and protects against personal bias.

No one can double-check everything that goes on, as the mind deals with inner feelings, perceptions of experience, and thought processes. Science brings the steps of inquiry out of the mind and into public view so that they can be shared as part of the process of accumulating knowledge.

The Role of Imagination, Custom, and Intuition

The mind, in its many ways of knowing, is never so clever or so mysterious as in the exercise of *imagination*. If there is any sense in which people can leap over tall obstacles at a single bound, it is in the flight of the mind. But it is one thing to imagine a possible proposition about reality, and it is quite another to start imagining evidence.

Science is really a matter of figuring out relationships between things we know something about. To propose a relationship is a creative and imaginative act, however much systematic preparation may lie in the background. To test a proposition against reality involves a different order of imagination—mainly the ability to find in the bits and pieces of information elicited from reality the one item that is essential to testing the credibility of a particular idea.

It is in the realm of discovery that science becomes a direct partner of imagination. The history of natural science is filled with examples, from the realization that the earth revolves around the sun, and not vice versa, to the discovery that matter is made up of tiny atoms. Each of these discoveries was made by bold and imaginative people who were not afraid to challenge a whole structure of customary belief by consulting evidence in the real world. Although these were discoveries on a grand scale, the same sort of effort is involved in stepping outside accepted explanations of human behavior to imagine other possibilities and test them by the intelligent use of evidence. Feminists do this when they examine traditional claims about male-female differences. To be truly imaginative is something like trying to escape gravity—the initial move is the hardest. Even though the social sciences have as yet few discoveries to compare with the feats of natural science, the application of science to social relations is a much more recent and vastly more complicated undertaking.[4]

[4]Perhaps one of the earliest attempts to confront social custom with science was the effort in the late nineteenth century by Francis Galton, an English scientist, to test the efficacy of prayer. Observing that prayers were daily offered in churches throughout the land for the long life of royalty, he compared their longevity to that of the gentry

At a fundamental level, scientific inquiry is motivated by curiosity and a desire to find order in what may seem to be chaos. We see an array of confusing events, incidents, and behavior and have an urge to know why something happened or what event caused another. Social science allows us to satisfy our curiosity and to gain understanding for its own sake. On another level, social science produces knowledge that is communicable and can be used to explain our understanding to others.

Whatever we may come to say about the careful thinking scientific analysis requires, there is still no way to capture completely the wondrous process of "having an idea." Science is absolutely *not* a system for frustrating that exercise of intuition and imagination; rather, it is a set of procedures for making such ideas as fruitful and productive as human ingenuity allows. Even the most wonderful idea, whatever its source, is only as good as its relationship to some present or potential reality. Science is the art of reality testing, of taking ideas and confronting them with observable evidence drawn from the phenomena to which they relate.

To step back from the general blur of human relationships and envision alternative possibilities demands a level of imagination that is as uncommon as it is necessary. In the usual run of social and political experience, David Hume's observation may be sadly accurate: "[People], once accustomed to obedience, never think of departing from that path in which they and their ancestors trod and to which they are confined by so many

and a variety of professionals. He found, after excluding deaths by accident or violence, and including only those who had survived their thirtieth year, that the average age of decease for royalty was 64.04 years, the lowest age for all his categories. Galton did observe, however, that prayer has many personal uses aside from the fulfillment of requests. And, who knows, royalty might have died even sooner but for such petitions. P. B. Medawar, *Induction and Intuition in Scientific Thought* (Philadelphia: American Philosophical Society, 1969), pp. 2–7.

urgent and visible motives."[5] Yet it is in the understanding and reform of social and political arrangements that the world requires the very best application of disciplined imagination. In the absence of imaginative efforts to understand the reality of society, we are confined to the beaten path of custom and the inequities that stifle human potential.

We also may be confined to some very unproductive habits of behavior. It used to be the custom in England to hang pickpockets publicly in order to discourage others in the trade. Someone noticed, however, that *more* pockets were picked at pickpocket hangings than at other public events. The custom has survived that bit of social science far longer than it should have.

Custom is not all bad, for it may embody the lessons learned from a long, often unhappy, experience with reality; and it is, in a vague way, scientific. Custom frequently holds communities together in the face of enormous and even violent pressures. Yet the task of any social science must be to understand why things are the way they are, as well as how the elements of social life can be reformed to allow for more humane patterns of personal development and expression. The weapons in this struggle for understanding are not only science with its procedures for disciplining inquiry but also the intuition that life can be better than it is, that a given pattern of behavior may be other than inevitable, that even the smallest transactions of behavior may contain the keys to larger structures of possiblity and potential.

The method of any effort at understanding involves a tension between thought and investigation. There are various ways of linking these two components. The mystic perceives an inner truth and interprets "signs" that he or she finds in

[5]"Of the Origin of Government," *Political Essays*, ed. Charles Hendel (New York: Liberal Arts Press, 1953), p. 41.

12

reality as symptoms of the validity of the insight. The historian looks for patterns in the past and, having conceptualized them, suggests their usefulness in interpreting the meanings of events. Thus the "rise of the middle class" in Europe becomes a major interpretive concept. Someone who is scientific attempts to be more concrete than the mystic and more precise than the historian with respect to the *thoughts* by which research is guided, the *data* regarded as significant in the investigation, and the *measures* used in testing mental constructions against reality.

In the chapters that follow, the steps involved in building scientific understanding will be taken one at a time. As you will see, the technique requires common sense more than technical knowledge or elaborate preparation.

CONCEPTS INTRODUCED

Science	Opinion
Technology	Objectivity
Communicable knowledge	Imagination
Valid knowledge	Custom
Compelling knowledge	Intuition
Reasoned judgment	

QUESTIONS FOR DISCUSSION

1. What are examples of nonscientific modes of understanding? Can you discuss how these nonscientific modes might be used to explain
    — why some nations are wealthier than others?
    — why political revolutions occur in some places but not in others?
    — who will win next year's World Series?

2. How is social scientific knowledge more powerful than other forms of knowledge (e.g., intuition, tradition)? What are its relative shortcomings?

3. How might scientific knowledge be useful to someone who is concerned with reforming or changing society?

4. Why is imagination essential to social science?

5. Is the application of imagination more important to social science than to natural science (e.g., chemistry, biology)?

OUTLINE

CHAPTER TWO

THE ELEMENTS OF SCIENCE

"[Scientific inquiry] begins as a story about a Possible World—a story which we invent and criticize and modify as we go along, so that it ends by being, as nearly as we can make it, a story about real life."

P. B. MEDAWAR

To see scientific thought in the context of other kinds of thinking, as we have tried to do, tells us why we should be interested in science. Now it is time to see what science is made of.

The elements of a scientific strategy are, in themselves, simple to understand. They are: concepts, variables, hypotheses, measurements, and theories. The way in which these are combined constitutes the scientific method. It is the function of theory to give meaning and motivation to this method by enabling us to interpret what is observed. First, we will try to put each element in place.

The Origin and Utility of Concepts

If you had to purge all words and other symbols from your mind and confront the world with a virgin mind, what would you do? Without a body to sustain, you might do nothing. The necessities of survival, however, start closing in, and the first act of the mind might be to sort out the edible objects from the inedible, then the warm from the cold, the friendly from the hostile. From there it isn't very far to forming concepts like *food, shelter, warmth* and symbolizing these concepts in the form of words or utterances. Thus, humbly, emerges the instrument called language. The search for truly usable concepts and categories is under way. Languages are nothing more than huge collections of names for things, feelings, and ideas generated or acquired by people in the course of relating to each other and to their environment.

Some concepts and classifications might not be very helpful. To conceptualize all plants under only a single designation would preclude further distinctions between those that are edible, those that heal, and those that poison. Some concepts relate to experience too vaguely: English has but one word for something so various and complicated as love. Greek allows three concepts: *eros* for romantic love, *agape* for generalized feelings of affection, and *filios* for family love. The inadequacy of English in dealing with the concept *love* affects everyone's experience through the tricky ways the word is used in our culture.

Notice that reality testing is built right into the process of naming things, one of the most elementary transactions of existence. That back-and-forth between the stimuli of the environment and the reflections of the mind makes up the kind of thought we will be trying to capture for analysis.

After several thousand years of history, we still have to face the fact that the process of naming things is difficult. Language emerges essentially by agreement. You and I and the other members of the family (tribe, state, nation, world) agree, for example, to call things that twinkle in the sky "stars." Unfortunately, these agreements may not be very precise. In common usage, the term "star" covers a multitude of objects, big and small, hot and cold, solid and gaseous.

To call a thing by a precise name is the beginning of understanding, because it is the key to the procedure that allows the mind to grasp reality and its many relationships. It makes a great deal of difference whether an illness is conceived of as caused by the Evil Spirit or by bacteria on a binge. The concept *bacteria* is tied to a system of concepts in which there is a connection to a powerful repertory of treatments, that is, antibiotics.

To capture meaning is language is a profound and subtle process, even if it is a little sloppy. For example, the abstract concept *race* expresses differences in the way that groups are identified. When names are given to categories or properties of race, the problems, power, and difficulty of naming things become evident. Researchers often name people "white" or "nonwhite" (or "Anglo" or "non-Anglo") when using simplistic classifications of race. Such a distinction, although common practice, trivializes differences among a large portion of the world's people. Also, the names themselves can raise complex issues. Think of the various names used in the United States to refer to African Americans (Negro, African American, person of color, black) or Hispanic Americans (Latino, Latina, Hispanic, person of color, Latin American, Mexican American, Central American, Puerto Rican, etc.).

Naming is a process that can give the namer great power. Properties of the concept *race* are not easily named. Names of races, moreover, confer different identities on different people. In your own expression of social scientific thinking, although you are invited to be precise about concepts, you are not invited to be arrogant about the utility of your new knowledge for reworking lives, societies, and civilizations.

The importance of having the right name for a thing can

hardly be overestimated. Thomas Hobbes, a seventeenth-century political theorist, thought the proper naming of things so important to the establishment of political order that he made it a central function of the sovereign. King James understood the message and ordered an authoritative translation of the Bible as a way of overcoming violent squabbles about the precise meanings of words in the Scriptures.

More germane to the modern scene, George Orwell, in his anti-utopian novel *1984*, gave us a vision of a whole bureaucracy devoted to reconstructing language concepts to enhance the power of a totalitarian society. In recent U.S. political history, President Reagan's press secretary would sometimes claim that, rather than lying, the President had "misspoken." These examples are intended to make you aware that by tinkering with the meanings of concepts, one can play with the foundations of human understanding and social control.

But it will be a while before you master the scientific method sufficiently to pull off anything very grand. For now, the point is that, for scientific purposes, concepts are: (1) tentative, (2) based on agreement, and (3) useful only to the degree that they capture or isolate some significant and definable item in reality.

What have concepts got to do with science? If you've spent any time around babies, you may notice that they often try to show off by pointing at things and naming them. It gets a little boring the tenth or fifteenth time through, but babies take justifiable pride in the exercise. Next come sentences. From naming things, from being able to symbolize something rather than simply pointing at it, comes the next step in moving reality around so it can produce things that are needed. The first sentence Andrew Hoover spoke was to his sister Erin. Sitting on a little cart he said, "Erin, push me!" She did.

What you are reading now is an effort to link concepts in order to expand your understanding. People speak sentences by the thousands in an attempt to move reality to some useful response. Most people don't have the good luck Andrew did on his first try. Often the concepts are confusing and the connections are vague or unlikely, not to mention the problem that the speaker has with the listener's perceptions and motives.

Thought and theory develop through the linking of concepts. Consider, as an example, Pierre Proudhon's famous proposition, "Property is theft!" Property, as a concept, stands for the notion that a person can claim sole ownership of land or other resources. Theft, of course, means the act of taking something without justification. By linking these two concepts through the verb "is," Proudhon meant to equate the institution of private property with the denial of humankind's common ownership of nature's resources. The concept of privately owned property was, he thought, unjustifiable thievery. While Proudhon's declaration illustrates the linkage of concepts at the lofty philosophical level, the humblest sentence performs the same operation.

Science is a way of checking on the formulation of concepts and testing the possible linkages between them through references to observable phenomena. The next step is to see how scientists turn concepts into something that can be observed. When concepts are defined as *variables*, they can be used to form a special kind of sentence, the *hypothesis*.

What Is a Variable?

A variable is a name for something that is thought to influence (or be influenced by) a particular state of being in something else. Heat is one variable in making water boil, and so is pressure. Age has been established as a modestly important variable in voting; however, there are many other more significant variables: socioeconomic standing, parental influence, race, gender, region of residence, and so on.

A variable is, in addition, a special kind of concept that

21

contains within it a notion of degree or differentiation. Temperature is an easily understood example of a variable. It includes
the notion of more or less heat, that is, of degree. As the name
suggests, variables are things that vary. Interesting questions in
social science center on concepts that involve variation and how
changes in one phenomenon help to explain variation in another. Consider, as an example, the relationship between religion and voting. In the first place, religion is a different kind of
variable than, say, temperature. Although there may be such a
thing as degrees of "religiosity,"[1] it is likely we would discuss
variation in the concept *religion* in terms of religious denomina-
tions. There is substantial variation in the religions with which
people identify. In an assessment of voting behavior in the 1992
presidential election, exit poll data collected by Voter Research
and Surveys found that fully 78 percent of Jewish voters selected Democrat Bill Clinton (compared to 12 percent for Republican George Bush and 10 percent for Ross Perot), whereas
44 percent of Catholic voters selected Clinton (compared to 36
percent for Bush and 20 percent for Perot).[2] Data such as these
permit us to say something meaningful about the relationship
between the variable *religion* and the variable *voting behavior.*

Although most variables deal with differences of degree, as
in temperature, or differences of variety, like religion, some
variables are even simpler. These deal with the most elementary kind of variation: present or absent, there or not there,
existent or nonexistent. Take pregnancy, for example. There is
no such thing as a little bit of it. Either the condition exists or it
doesn't.

---

[1]Various attempts have been made to measure degree of individual "religiosity" in
terms of attitudinal and behavioral traits such as regularity of church attendance. For an
example, see Lyman A. Kellstedt and Mark A. Noll, "Religion, Voting for President, and
Party Identification, 1948–1984," *Religion and American Politics: From the Colonial
Period to the 1980s,* ed. Mark A. Noll (Oxford: Oxford University Press, 1990), p. 347.

[2]"The 1992 Elections," *New York Times,* November 5, 1992, p. B9.

Turning concepts into variables, dull as it may seem, is a very creative process and often raises intriguing questions. Consider, as an illustration, such an ordinary variable as time. The early Greeks puzzled a good deal over how to conceptualize this variable. It seems obvious that time has to be thought of as having a beginning—so philosophers went about trying to figure out when the beginning was. Yet the nagging question always popped up—What happened before that? Plato and Aristotle both played with the idea that time might not be linear at all; that is, it might *not* have a beginning, a progression, and presumably an end. It just might be cyclical! This seems crazy to us children of linear time, but they were thinking that universal time might be something like the cycle of the body, a rhythm found everywhere in nature. Historic time, therefore, might best be conceived of as an unfolding structure of events in which one follows the other until the whole pattern is played out and the entire cycle starts over again. Aristotle commented that it just might be that he himself "was living *before* the Fall of Troy quite as much as *after* it, since, when the wheel of fortune had turned through another cycle, the Trojan War would be re-enacted and Troy would fall again."[3]

The social science done by introductory students seldom involves such mind-boggling conceptual problems, yet it wouldn't do to pretend that these problems don't exist. The variable *personality*, for example, is reputed to have more than four hundred definitions in the professional literature, partly because personality is a compound of a huge range of other variables: class, status, self-concept, race, socialization, and so forth. The complexity of personality as a variable has driven social scientists to such awkward definitions as: "One's

[3]Stephen Toulmin and June Goodfield, *The Discovery of Time* (New York: Harper & Rowe, 1965), p. 46.

acquired, relatively enduring, yet dynamic, unique system of predispositions to psychological and social behavior."[4]

Even when social scientists agree on the description of a variable, that doesn't mean the definition possesses the qualities of eternal truth—it just means that some people who have thought about it carefully agree that a given definition seems to help answer some questions. Moreover, researchers often settle on a definition of a variable for reasons of convenience. Party identification in the United States is conventionally measured by the response to a survey question that places voters on a continuum such as this:

←strong Dem——weak Dem——Ind leaning Dem——
Ind——Ind leaning Rep——weak Rep——strong Rep→

Political independents are assumed to be in the center of the political spectrum. Yet the truth of the matter might be that many "Independents" think of themselves as radicals who are outside the center. Some might be so apolitical that they just don't think of themselves in terms of political parties at all. Furthermore, some "leaning" independents are more partisan in their voting than are "weak" partisans.[5] Although this definition of the variable might not perfectly reflect the underlying truth of the concept *partisanship,* it continues to have predictive power. Since the question has been asked on surveys for decades, it allows researchers to evaluate trends in partisanship over time. As the difficulties of categorizing independents on this spectrum become apparent, new definitions of partisanship will emerge. Ignoring the problem of specifying how concepts

---

[4]Gordon DiRenzo, *Personality and Politics* (Garden City, N.Y.: Anchor Books, 1974), p. 16.
[5]William Flannigan and Nancy Zingalle, *Political Behavior of the American Electorate,* 7th ed. (Washington, D.C.: Congressional Quarterly Press, 1991), pp. 49–54.

should be turned into variables doesn't make the problem go away, it just gets you further into the linguistic soup.

The huge stock of concepts in language creates enormous possibilities for linking up variables to explain events. People have muddled around for centuries trying to sort through significant connections. Science is a slightly elevated form of muddling by which these connections are tried out and tested as carefully as possible. In medical science, it took centuries to isolate the many variables affecting disease. Only recently has medical science become so disciplined that it can diagnose many diseases through highly significant blood-chemistry analysis. This development represents the present stage of a long process of isolating and eliminating a host of unimportant or marginally significant variables. Western doctors have recently come up against an ancient form of medicine developed to a high art in China, and now we have medical scientists trying to figure out why acupuncture works. Whole new sets of variables must be considered, new conceptual bridges built, and the resistance of conventional understanding overcome.

Unfortunately for *social* science, we have barely figured out how to lay the foundation for a structure of theory to explain social behavior. Many new students of social science do not see—especially when confronted by thick texts in introductory courses—the context of struggle and accomplishment, tentativeness and probability, behind what has been achieved in social understanding.

Social science currently contains many subdivisions (e.g., political science, sociology, economics, psychology, education), all of which are working on defining, observing, and linking specific variables within subsystems of behavior. Social scientists are in the process of chasing a good many possible connections between variables. The bits of tested knowledge that do emerge await an integration across the lines of these inquiries. Relatively few have been attempted, though these efforts are bound to increase in view of the dramatic need for comprehensive social understanding.

Quantification and Measurement: Turning Concepts into Variables

We said earlier that social scientists turn concepts into variables. This is done so the concept can be expressed in a form that is observable and includes some notion of degree or differentiation. The next question is: How does one pin down that degree or differentiation? The answer involves a two-step process: quantification and measurement.

The idea of *quantification* means setting up a standard amount of a thing and putting a label on it. When we do this, we make it possible to express abstract concepts (such as length) in a manner that provides a common reference for observation. The origins of some quantifications are pretty strange. The ancient Greeks, for example, needed a standard quantity of distance, so they settled on the length of Hercules' foot. For a long time the foot competed with the cubit, which was the length of someone else's forearm. The trouble with the cubit was that people could never agree on how long the standard forearm was—some said 17 inches, some said 21 inches. Consequently, we don't hear much about cubits anymore.

Isolating standardized units increases the power of description and analysis. When Gabriel Fahrenheit established the idea of a degree of temperature, he made possible a much more useful description of hot and cold. It makes a considerable difference with respect to a puddle of water if the temperature is 32 degrees rather than 33 degrees; the words "cold" and "colder" don't work very well for capturing that vital degree of difference.

Quantification in social science takes two forms: discrete and continuous. *Discrete quantification relates to counting the presence or absence of a thing. It also relates to counting differences of quality as they are captured in categories.* A vote for a candidate is a discrete and specific act that can be counted in a conventional manner. A person's sex is a quality that can usually be counted as being either male or female.

Some quantifications, however, have to capture the notion of variation along a continuum. Age is an example of a continuous quantification. True, one can count the number of years in a person's age, but the quantification of age is an expression of something that is ongoing. One of the authors of this book is 53.27 years old today; next Saturday he will be 53.29 years old. *Continuous quantification deals not with discrete items but with dimensions like age, length, and time. The mark of continuous quantification is that the variable involved may have any value on a scale,* whereas in discrete quantification only whole numbers appear (as in counting sheep).

Each variable has its own peculiar problems and potentials for quantification. One of the distinguishing characteristics of a well-developed science is the array of quantifiable variables that are useful to people working in the field. One of the marks of a smart scientist is the ability to find ways of quantifying important variables in a reliable and meaningful way. Economics has come a long way by using money as a unit of analysis (though economists, among others, sometimes confuse money with value). Many powerful economic indicators, such as the gross national product or the consumer price index, are based on money.

Unfortunately for the other social sciences, there aren't such easily quantifiable units for measuring power or representing psychological stress, alienation, happiness, personal security, or, for that matter, value. Yet inventive scientists have found more or less successful ways of capturing quantifiable pieces of these variables. A text in any of these areas contains dozens of illustrations of how concepts are turned into quantifiable variables, and we will see some of them in the next chapter. The importance of quantification is that when it can be accomplished, there is potential for more precise measurement.

Measurement is not something we choose to do or not do—it is inherent in every analytic discussion. If you doubt this, listen carefully in the next conversation you have and notice your dependence on terms that imply measurement. A simple political statement such as, "Democrats generally favor the poor," involves measurement. The verb "favor" implies degrees of difference, and so does the term "poor." The modifier "generally" is an attempt to qualify the measurement by indicating that it is not a universal characteristic of all Democrats.

If quantities can be established, measurement becomes much easier. The most obvious measurement deals with the problem of *how much:* how much distance, how much money, and so forth. Some questions of how much are not so easy to measure—public opinion, for example. Using responses to questions as the quantifiable unit of analysis, one crude survey technique provides respondents a "forced choice" and divides opinion into favorable versus unfavorable. Here, opinion is quantified as a discrete, categorical variable. "Are you for it or against it?" Public-opinion polling is usually done on this basis. One thing such a simple measurement conceals, of course, is the intensity of the opinion. On many political issues there may be minorities that are passionately on one side and a majority that is lukewarmly on the other side. Some public-opinion polls deal with this by using four categories instead of two:

Strongly For   For   Against   Strongly Against

An even fancier way of addressing the problem is to measure opinion in terms of degree. Some surveys ask people to evaluate candidates or parties on a "feeling thermometer" scale where 0 is negative, 50 is neutral, and 100 is positive.[6] This helps expand the range of responses and reveals more acurately the state of opinion. A political system that simply acts on majority sentiment without taking intensity into account can get itself into a lot of trouble—as this nation did over the Vietnam War. A passionate minority of opponents became embittered and alienated by the reliance of policy makers on a rather unenthusiastic majority of supporters.

Validity and Reliability of Variables

Quantified measurement of variables, properly conceived and executed, has the potential for specifying differentiation and degree more effectively than fuzzy words in vague sentences. However we decide to measure variables, we hope to find a method of counting that would provide *reliable* results if it were used by other researchers.

As an example, we could decide to measure "presidential approval" by asking a random sample of respondents if they "like" or "dislike" the president, thereby forcing a choice between only two alternatives. We might expect that other researchers could use the same measure the next day with a comparable random sample and produce results similar to ours.

Conversely, we might ask the first four people we see on a bus to "discuss what they think" about the president. We could then rate presidential approval based on our personal *impression* of their responses. Other researchers using this measure

---

[6]Problems with "forced choice" measures are discussed in Christopher Hitchens, "Voting in the Passive Voice," *Harper's,* April 1992, pp. 45–52. For examples of "thermometer" measures of opinion, see Martin Wattenberg, "Negativity or Neutrality," *The Decline of American Political Parties* (Cambridge, Mass.: Harvard University Press, 1990).

the next day on the same bus might produce wildly different results. The answers may be vague, and the values influencing the interpretation may differ.

Measurement of a variable is said to be *reliable* if it produces the same result when different people use it. The forced-choice question would probably produce consistent results, because each researcher using comparable samples simply has to count up the number of "likes" and "dislikes" to find a measure of approval. Open-ended discussions with people on the bus, however, require that the researcher interpret a variety of comments that might (or might not) reflect approval. The answers are meaningful—in some ways even more meaningful—than the forced-choice responses. But they are less likely to get us a reliable answer to the question of presidential popularity.

Theoretical concerns about measures of variables can be subtle. Each measure we use is supposed to do a good job of representing the underlying truth of the abstract concept we claim to be representing with a quantified variable. A measure is said to be *valid* "if it does what it is intended to do."[7] The closer a quantified measure comes to reflecting the truth of the underlying concept the research is concerned with, the more valid a measure is. One of the difficulties of social science is that there is never any clear way of directly assessing validity. For example, the IQ test is a measure that might be used reliably by many researchers attempting to quantify intelligence. However, it will always be debatable just how accurately this test measures a concept as rich, varied, and powerful as intelligence. IQ tests may be reliable, but are they entirely valid?

Improperly conceived measurement is dangerous precisely because it can be so powerful. A tragic and repugnant

[7]Edward G. Carmines and Richard Zeller, "Reliability and Validity Assessment," *Sage University Paper Series on Quantitative Applications in the Social Sciences,* no. 17 (Beverly Hills, Calif.: Sage Press, 1979).

example was the use of "body counts" as a key to "progress" in the U.S. effort in Vietnam. Newscasts about the war would usually report the military's figures on how many "enemies" were killed each day. The implication was that the more we killed, the faster we would win the war. There were two things wrong with this quantified measurement.

First, it didn't measure what some policy makers alleged that it measured: the amount of success or failure in achieving overall objectives in the war. Since the war was at least as much a political and psychological struggle as a military conflict, the body counts were largely useless as an index of success. They may have told the military something about the condition of the enemy, but reliance on them promoted adverse political and psychological effects in the Vietnamese population and in our own. The Vietnamese began to notice that it was mainly people of their own race and nationality who were being killed by Americans, regardless of whatever else the war was about. Americans thus came to be feared rather than welcomed as allies by many Vietnamese. At the same time, we began to see ourselves as technological warriors wreaking havoc in a poor country.

A second flaw in the measurement was its implementation. Troops in the field were supposed to count enemy dead and report the number. However, several factors intervened: the confusion (sometimes deliberate) about who was the enemy, the error introduced by having more than one person counting in a particular location, and the chain-of-command pressures for a high body count. Consequently, while the body counts kept going up and led to predictions of success in the war, the actual situation deteriorated.[8]

The very important point is that sloppy or inappropriate measurement is generally worse than no measurement at all. In-

---

[8]During the Persian Gulf War, the allied military command avoided these problems by not announcing estimates of Iraqi casualties.

terpreting the results of measurement requires an understanding of the measurement itself. In Chapter Five, we explore the practical steps involved in making and interpreting measurements.

The Hypothesis

Although much of the preceding discussion may have seemed like a serial review of bits and pieces of scientific thinking, a discussion of hypotheses will bring these matters together.

A hypothesis is a sentence of a particularly well-cultivated breed. The purpose of a hypothesis is to organize a study. If the hypothesis is carefully formed, all the steps of the scientific method follow, as does an outline for the project, a bibliography, a list of resources needed, and a specification of the measures appropriate to the study. The hypothesis provides the structure.

A hypothesis proposes a relationship between two or more variables. For example: *Political participation* INCREASES with *education*. This simple assertion can be seen as a hypothesis. It has a subject (the variable, *political participation*), a connective verb (a relationship, INCREASES), and an object (the variable, *education*).

To illustrate the point further:

> *Alienation* INCREASES with *poverty.*
> *Union members* are MORE LIKELY than nonunion members to *vote Democratic.*

Or, less obviously (and, for exercise, you can identify the variables and relations):

> Absence makes the heart grow fonder.
> An apple a day keeps the doctor away.
> Early to bed, early to rise, makes people healthy, wealthy, and
>   wise.

It is crucial to realize that a hypothesis is a *supposition,* as the *Oxford English Dictionary* points out, "which serves as a starting point for further investigation by which it may be proved or disproved. . . ." A hypothesis stands near the beginning, not the end, of a study, although good studies may suggest new paths of fruitful inquiry and new hypotheses.

So far, most of our examples of hypotheses have been quite simple. But to go from the straightforward to the bizarre, let us cite an experience in teaching scientific thinking. A student came to one of us with the following proposal for research:

> The fragile psycho-pathological type of double helical existence issuing from the precarious relationship of the colonizer and the colonized (which figuratively is similar to the relationship of Siamese twins) and their respective interaction within the colonial situation is psychologically effective, which ramifications lead to psychological maladjustments, i.e., neuroses which subsequently define the nature of the political particulars therein.

That was just the beginning of the proposal! In all that confusing language, there are lots of variables and many relationships. Sorting it out, however, yields two hypotheses. We cut it down to:

> *Colonialism* IS ASSOCIATED WITH *neurotic behavior by colonizer and colonial.*
>
> *This neurotic behavior* INFLUENCES *the political structure of colonialism.*

These two hypotheses, large as they are, were somewhat manageable. The concept *colonialism* describes a well-established political situation. The relationship IS ASSOCIATED WITH was a retreat from saying CAUSES—a precaution taken in view of the limited research resources available to the student. *Neurotic behavior* is a tricky concept, but it has parentage in the literature of psychoanalytic theory; there are behaviors that can respectably be labeled neurotic. From there it becomes a matter of showing the links between the kinds of neurotic, self-destructive behavior that occur in colonial situations and the repressive and authoritarian patterns of colonial politics.

Had the student accomplished all that these hypotheses imply by way of evidence gathering, measurement, and evaluation, he would have been in line for a Ph.D. As long as we both knew that he was just scratching the surface, his paper (bravely entitled "Colonialism: A Game for Neurotics") was good enough for undergraduate requirements.

One of the things this example illustrates is that there is often a prior step to hypothesis formation. The step is called *problem reformulation.* In the preceding example, we began with a generalized concern about colonialism and neurosis. The student elaborated that concern into a complex description of the problem. We narrowed it down by specifying variables and relationships into something that could be dealt with, at least in a general way. With a workable reformulation, defining the ways that variables are represented becomes easier.

One of the arts of social science is skillful problem reformulation. Reformulation requires, in addition to some analytic common sense, the ability to see the variables in a situation and the possible relationship between them. A good first step is to break the problem into its component variables and relationships. Writing down lists of hypotheses associated with a problem enables you to select the ones that answer two questions: Which hypotheses are crucial to the solution of the whole problem? For which hypotheses is there information within the range of your resources? Sometimes these questions force some unpleasant choices, but they help prevent arriving at the end of a research effort with nothing substantial on which to hang a conclusion. The preceding example on colonialism and neurosis illustrates the point.

The importance of establishing a hypothesis correctly before starting off on a research task can hardly be overestimated. The following rules will help:

1. The *variables* must be clearly specified and measurable by some technique you know how to use.
2. The *relationship* between the variables must be precisely stated and measurable.
3. The hypothesis should be *testable* so that evidence of the relationship can be observed, demonstrated, or falsified.

If these rules are not followed, the hypothesis may be unwieldy, ridiculous, or just too hard to research in view of available resources. Precise definitions and thoughtful specification of measurements are, in short, the keys.

The struggle to form a hypothesis carefully may not be enjoyable, but the questions raised in the process have to be answered sooner or later.

The hypothesis, then, provides the structure for your entire research effort, whether it involves interviews and surveys, the analysis of previously collected data, library research, or all three. It will direct you to relevant information so you do not waste time and effort. The variables you have selected can be researched through library card catalogues, book indexes, periodical guides, on-line services and CD-ROM/computer data-base searches. The relationships proposed between the variables suggest the measurement tools and standards for evaluation that you will need to use. The results of the hypothesis test are the substance of your conclusions.

Once relationships between variables have been established through hypothesis formation and testing, these relationships can be expressed as *generalizations*. Generalizations based on tested relationships are the object of science. A generalization is a hypothesis affirmed by testing. As generalizations in a field of study accumulate, they form the raw stuff of theories. But this gets us ahead of the story. For now, we need to see how the scientific method sets the procedure for research into a logical sequence.

The Scientific Method

The technique known as the scientific method is quite commonsensical. The model inquiry proceeds by steps that include:

1. The identification of the *variables* to be studied
2. A *hypothesis* about the relation of one variable to another or to a situation
3. A *reality test* whereby the hypothetical relationship is measured and compared with results that would demonstrate the absence of a relationship
4. An *evaluation* in which the measured relationship is compared with the original hypothesis, and *generalizations* are developed
5. *Suggestions* about the theoretical significance of the findings, factors involved in the test that may have distorted the results, and other hypotheses that the inquiry brings to mind

Although we have sketched here the bare bones of the scientific method, the actual procedure of research does not always start directly with hypothesis formation. As a preliminary to stating hypotheses, social scientists often examine the data collected in a subject area to see if there are connections between the variables. The relationships brought to light by various statistical processes frequently suggest the hypotheses it would be fruitful to explore. Occasionally, simply getting involved with a set of data triggers an interesting thought, a chance insight, or a new idea. A great quantity of data has been generated over the past few decades, so researchers can usually avoid having to begin at the beginning with every inquiry. The analysis of existing data can be extremely helpful in identifying new data needed to test a crucial relationship.

This is only an outline of the scientific method. In the hands of a skilled analyst, other elements are introduced, such as the use of alternative forms of measuring results, detailed conceptual analysis of the variable description, relationships between one's own study and others, assessments of the validity of the measuring instruments, the use of experimental and control groups, and, equally important, careful conjecture that goes beyond what is established in the test itself. These embellishments on the methodology, however, relate more to the tools used in carrying on the method than to the method itself.

The point is that *the scientific method seeks to test thoughts against observable evidence in a disciplined manner, with each step in the process made explicit.*

Consider the differences between two kinds of studies: (1) An empirical scientific study in which the author states his or her values, forms hypotheses, lays out a testing procedure, carefully selects and discusses measurements, produces a specific result, and relates this to the hypotheses. (2) A nonscientific study in which the author expresses values, develops a general thesis, examines relevant examples, and states the conclusions.

Notice that the tension between thought and investigation is present in both studies. But one important difference is the feasibility of checking the validity of the conclusions in the first example as opposed to the second, by repeating the study. *Replication* is the word social scientists use to indicate the ability to repeat a study as a way of checking on its validity. Replication constitutes a very strong test of a good study because it can reveal errors that might have crept in through the procedures and evaluative judgments contained in the principal study.

A second difficulty with a nonscientific study lies in the

problem of relating one study to another. Have you ever been annoyed in a discussion when someone asks you to "define your terms"? Have you ever gotten into arguments that end with, "How do you know that is true?" A good scientific study presents all the information needed to see what took place. For example, if standard variable definitions are used, a study of voters' assessments of candidates can be added to studies of how voters view issues, parties, or whatever. As scientists try to build cumulative bodies of knowledge, different studies of the same variables using different measures can be compared to see if measurement techniques create alternative results. The point, once again, is that science regulates and specifies the relationship between thought and investigation in such a way that others may know exactly what has been done.

The Many Roles of Theory

Science rests its claim to authority upon its firm basis in observable evidence about something called "reality." We have occasionally described science as, simply, reality testing. Since everybody thinks he or she knows what reality is, science acquires a fundamental appeal. Yet the necessary partner of realism in science is that wholly imaginary phenomenon, *theory.* Without the many roles that theory plays, there would be no science (and, some would argue, there would be no understandable "reality," either).

Just as language arises out of the experience of coming to grips with human needs, so also does theory arise from tasks that people face. The hardest task is to explain what's really going on out there. Volumes have been written about what theory is and isn't. For our purposes, a theory is a set of related propositions that suggest why events occur in the manner that they do.

The propositions that make up theories are of the same

form as hypotheses: they consist of concepts and the linkages or relationships between them. Theories are built up as hypotheses are tested and new relationships emerge.

Theory abounds in the most ordinary transactions of life. There are theories of everything from the payoff of pinball machines to the inner meaning of *Peanuts* cartoons. The grandest theories of all are religious and philosophical, embracing huge orders of questions about the origin of the physical universe, the history of the species, the purposes of life, and the norms of behavior that lead to virtue and, possibly, happiness. To the faithful, such theories are made true by a belief in supernatural phenomena. These kinds of theories are presented as if they were embedded in the larger cosmos of our existence awaiting our arrival at understanding.

Social science, by contrast, generally operates from a different perspective on theory. The most conventional posture of a social scientist is one of pragmatism: a theory is only as good as its present and potential uses in explaining observations. The point of any science is to develop a set of theories to explain the events within their range of observation.

It is tempting, but misleading, to conceive of theory as something rocklike and immobile behind the whiz and blur of daily experience. Rather, theory is a sometimes ingenious creation of human beings in their quest for understanding. People create theories in proportion to needs, and the theories they create can be either functional or dysfunctional to those needs. A theory could contain a complete system of categories and generalizations—but still be useless. If, for example, one were to categorize the world in terms of tall things and short things and characterize all the relationships between them, a theory would have been born, but it would be one of dubious utility—not false, but useless.

Social science theory is often derived from fundamental assumptions about human behavior. "Rational actor" theories are currently in vogue among many social scientists. These theories suggest that individuals, organizations, and nation-states are motivated by a desire to maximize their material interests. Based on this type of theory, we might hypothesize that voters select candidates that further their own economic interest. Alternatively, "psychological" theories assume that voting actions are determined by people's long-term feelings of attachment for political parties. Voters are thought to be socialized, via the family, to be loyal to a particular party. From this theory, we might hypothesize that voters act like their parents, or that they select candidates of the same party year after year. The origins of wars have been explained by rational actor theories and psychological theories, as well as by Marxian theories and other forms of social theory.

We have been discussing what theory is and is not. The next question is: What does it do? The answer is: many things. We will list four particular uses of theory in social scientific thinking:

1. Theory provides *patterns* for the interpretation of data.
2. Theory *links* one study with another.
3. Theory supplies frameworks within which concepts and variables acquire *special significance.*
4. Theory allows us to interpret the *larger meaning* of our findings for ourselves and others.

Let's see if we can illustrate these four uses of theory by looking at a single study of race and politics. Differences in the experiences of blacks and whites in the U.S. political system have left many unresolved questions about racial variations in political participation. One significant issue concerns the connection between access to power through officeholding and levels of participation. In an article on race, political orientation, and empowerment, Lawrence Bobo and Franklin Gilliam, Jr., reported the following results of a sample survey of American adults (see Table 2.1).[9] Empowerment refers to having achieved significant political representation in a community. The authors compared political orientations of blacks and whites, and then probed further to determine whether attitudes differed in cities with significant numbers of black officeholders.

What is the message of these data? Concentrating on the first two rows of data only, we find that race seems to have an influence on the orientation people have to politics—whether they are engaged, discontented, obedient, or alienated. Blacks in this sample appear to be somewhat less politically engaged and obedient, and more discontented and alienated, than whites.

Where does theory enter in? What theories fit this *pattern* of data? It seems that people like to think in terms of images, analogies, and patterns; this helps to simplify complex realities and to lighten the burden of thought. The usual theories of race and political orientation involve the historic difference in the treatment of blacks and whites by the political system.

The authors, wanting to go beyond conventional generalizations, *link* this study with previous research to suggest that a significant theoretical consideration is the degree of empowerment that blacks feel with respect to the political system.[10] Whites are accustomed to the notion that they can be represented in political offices by someone of their own race;

[9]From "Race, Sociopolitical Participation, and Black Empowerment," *American Political Science Review* 84, no. 2 (June 1990):377–393. The sample consisted of 1,466 English-speaking adults plus a black over-sample of 353 to bring the total black sample size to 544. Sample source: National Opinion Research Center General Social Survey, 1987, James Davis and Tom Smith, principal investigators.

[10]See Rufus Browning, Dale Rogers Marshall, and David H. Tabb, *Protest Is Not Enough: The Struggle of Blacks and Hispanics for Equality in Urban Politics* (Berkeley, Calif.: University of California Press, 1984).

TABLE 2.1 POLITICAL ORIENTATION AND EMPOWERMENT AMONG U.S. BLACKS AND WHITES, 1987

Political Orientation[a] (%)	Engaged	Discontented	Obedient	Alienated	Total (%)	Total No.
By Race[b]						
Blacks	25	20	22	32	99	531
Whites	42	12	26	19	99	1208
By Race and Black Empowerment[c]						
Blacks in:						
Low-empowerment cities	22	21	21	36	100	350
High-empowerment cities	32	18	24	26	100	181

[a]The four items listed result from combinations of responses to two indicators in the survey, one of political efficacy (the sense that one can have an influence on politics) and political trust (the feeling that leaders are reliable). *Engaged* = positive efficacy and trust; *discontented* = positive efficacy and negative trust; *obedient* = negative efficacy and positive trust; and *alienated* = negative efficacy and trust.
[b]$X^2 = 70.87$, d.f. $= 3$, $p < .001$.
[c]$X^2 = 9.71$, d.f. $= 3$, $p < .05$.

SOURCE: Table 5, from the article "Race, Sociopolitical Participation, and Black Empowerment," *American Political Science Review*, L. Bobo and F. Gilliam, Jr., 84:2, June 1990.

for blacks this is a much more recent experience (the number of black elected officials increased from 103 in 1964 to 6,384 in 1986).[11] Earlier studies did not take the empowerment factor into account.[12] It is a concept that has broad significance for democratic theory generally and "rational action" theories in particular. Empowerment causes the perceived benefits of participation to outweigh the costs. Participation levels for other groups that feel institutionally and politically marginalized might well reflect a similar response to empowerment. Through this link, the study aims to move social scientists to accumulate knowledge of relationships between different theoretical constructs.

So far we have seen two uses of theory in relation to this study: the *patterns* theory provides, and the ways that theory *links* one study to another.

The third use of theory is now apparent. The authors decided to test the *special significance* of empowerment by analyzing the difference in political orientation of blacks in cities where blacks had gained elective office, as opposed to those where whites remained in control. The results may be found in the second two rows of Table 2.1. Blacks living in communities with significant numbers of black officeholders are somewhat more engaged and less alienated than those who have reason to feel less empowered.[13] A realistic prospect of achieving power is associated with higher levels of engagement.

The *larger meaning* of these findings for theories relating

---

[11]Data from Eddie N. Williams and Milton D. Morris, cited in Bobo and Gilliam, "Race, Sociopolitical Participation . . . ," p. 377.

[12]See specif. Sidney Verba and Norman Nie, *Participation in America* (New York: Harper, 1972). Cf. Browning, Marshall, and Tabb, *Protest Is Not Enough*.

[13]It is interesting that black political empowerment does not have a statistically significant impact on *white* political orientations in the same communities. Cf. Bobo and Gilliam, "Race, Sociopolitical Participation . . . ," p. 385.

to empowerment and to race in politics is obvious. Participation in a representative democracy is not just a matter of having the formal right to vote. There also needs to be a way of identifying with the results of the process; participation is a matter of motivation and engagement as well as formal rights. There are clearly other factors involved, but empowerment does have a measureable effect on political orientation.

In discussing theory, we have presented a general outline of its commonplace uses in social scientific research. What we cannot capture is the subtlety and creativity with which people think about what they are observing. We can only say, on the one hand, that without theory social science would be an incoherent and meaningless pile of observations, data, and statistics. On the other hand, not all social science can be tied to rigorous and specific theoretical formulations. However, it is absolutely clear that complex social problems need all the well-informed study we can develop. The organization and evaluation of that knowledge in theoretical form is almost as important as gathering it in the first place. History is littered with the wreckage of poorly conceived social theories.

We now have in hand the basic tools of scientific thinking. But tools, by themselves, don't get the job done. We need a plan or, as described in the next chapter, a *strategy* for putting those tools to work to produce some knowledge.

CONCEPTS INTRODUCED

Concept
Variable
Discrete quantification
Continuous quantification
Measurement
Reliability
Validity

Hypothesis
Problem reformulation
Generalization
Scientific method
Replication
Theory

QUESTIONS FOR DISCUSSION

1. Consider the concept *unemployment.*
   a. How can it be given a definition so that it can be measured as a variable?
   b. How many definitions of unemployment can you think of?
   c. How do these definitions differ?

2. Evaluate different measures of unemployment in terms of reliability and validity.
   a. In terms of reliability, if other researchers used your measures (variables), would they produce similar results?
   b. In terms of validity, do the measures do a good job of representing the concept *unemployment*?

3. One of the more complex questions that social scientists deal with is: Why do people rebel? Consider three examples of major revolutions (seventeenth-century England, eighteenth-century France, early-twentieth-century Russia). Based on these examples, can you form some hypotheses about why revolutions occur? When forming your hypotheses, consider the following:
   — What variables are associated with the occurrence of revolutions?
   — How do you define concepts such as *revolution*?
   — Is your definition something that other researchers could apply reliably to other nations in which revolutions have or have not occurred?
   — How are the variables in your hypotheses linked together?
   — How would you test the hypotheses?
   — Would another person reach the same conclusion as you if he or she used your measures and the tests you suggest?

OUTLINE

    I. *Thinking Over the Problem*
        A. *Focus*
        B. *Hypothesis Formation*
        C. *Operationalizing Concepts*
   II. *Reality Testing*
        A. *Organizing the Bibliography*
        B. *Doing Research*
        C. *Analyzing the Results*
 III. *Understanding the Results*
        A. *Evaluating Concept Operationalization*
           and Variable Measurement
        B. *Were the Measures Any Good?*
        C. *Can Statistics Be Trusted?*
        D. *How Do Your Findings Fit with Theories in the Field?*

CHAPTER THREE

STRATEGIES

"At the most fundamental level, knowledge is organized experience and the search for knowledge is a search for patterns of organization. The organization is always created and not discovered."

EUGENE MEEHAN

Observant readers will notice that two words, usually thought to be integral to the scientific method, rarely appear in this book. They are "fact" and "truth." What both words have in common is an air of absolutism that misleads those who become involved in the scientific approach to learning. "Fact" means, according to its word root, "a thing done." That things do get done is not disputed, but the trouble is that "things done" are perceived not by some neutral omnipotent observer, but by people. People have limited powers of perception and structures of instinct and interest that influence how they see the world. *Science is a process for making these perceptions as explicit and open to examination as possible.* But the results of scientific procedure must always be taken as just that, an *attempt* to control a process that our very humanity makes difficult, if not impossible, to control totally.

For working purposes, social scientists generaly regard a fact as "a particular ordering of reality in terms of a theoretical interest."[1] Anything identified as a fact is tied to the particular interests the observer brings to the study of the phenomenon. Further than that we cannot usefully go, for a philosophical forest looms in which subtle questions are raised about whether a tree that falls unobserved has really fallen, since we can't know that it did.

The term "truth" is red meat for philosophers, and they are welcome to it. Science prefers to operate in the less lofty region of *falsifiable statements* that can be checked by someone else. Every good scientific proposition or generalization is stated in such a way that subsequent observations may provide either supporting evidence or evidence that raises questions about the accuracy of the proposition. By making the degree of verification a permanent consideration in science, a good many rash conclusions can be avoided.

"What, then, are we to believe in?" might be the response to this noncommittal attitude toward fact and truth. If you want something absolute to believe in, it must be found outside of science. Science is a working procedure for answering questions through the refinement of experience. Scientists may develop theories of awe-inspiring power, but the way such theories meet our very human needs for belief is a personal matter separate from the meaning of science for inquiry. To "believe in science" means no more nor less than to be committed to judgments based on reality testing rather than on some other kind of evidence or mental process.

You are now familiar with basic elements of science, such

---

[1]David Easton, *The Political System* (New York: Knopf, 1953), p. 53.

as variables, measurements, and hypotheses. In this chapter we will concentrate on how to shape ideas about the world into a form that allows for reality testing. Then the process of reality testing will be broken down into its parts. Finally, we will see what evaluative steps need to be taken for understanding the results of research.

The following remarks are designed as a step-by-step guide to scientific analysis. However, it must be realized that we are trying to capture only the most significant aspects of scientific procedure, not the finer points or the intricacies a sophisticated researcher would want to introduce. The following chapter, entitled "Refinements," adds to each element some ideas for increasing the power of your research strategy.

Please bear in mind that all we are doing here is regulating what is natural to human thought: a tension between thought and reality testing. So this chpater is organized into three sections: Thinking Over the Problem, Reality Testing, and Understanding the Results.

Thinking Over the Problem

The biggest challenge in doing research occurs at the very beginning. Once you have met that challenge, other steps fall into place. This is the problem of limiting the topic, or, more positively, of selecting an approach to the topic that will most efficiently get at the thing you want to understand. Most students have had the experience of writing a long, rambling, poorly focused paper. As the need for conclusions looms with the final pages, there occasionally arises the awful feeling that from what has been said reasonably and with evidence, little that is useful can be firmly concluded. The reason for such an inglorious end usually can be found in the beginning.

Focus

Since most of us are not trained to think in terms of formulating our ideas into hypotheses and testing them, it is best to start writing things down in the way they occur to the mind: as a sequence of ideas, thoughts, and notions. Ask yourself, Why am I interested in this? What is it that I am really after? See what happens. You may start with a broad topic:

> This country is in big trouble. Most people neither know nor care enough to choose a real leader—they just go for whoever looks good on television. Politics is such a joke.

Big subjects, but there is a theme here about whether modern democracy works or not.

At this stage it is a good idea to try to capture these thoughts in a paragraph or two. Get it on paper! Some general reading is a good idea. It helps to map out the areas of investigation. Too much reading may be a bad idea. Don't try to get into your actual research until you have thought through the larger frame of the problem.

Suppose you wind up with two paragraphs like this:

> Our leaders are getting elected for all the wrong reasons—like whether they are attractive or can sell themselves in the media. People buy into these phony appeals and don't really look at what they are getting.
> A person who is really honest and well prepared for the job could never get elected if s/he weren't a media star. Most of the people I talk to don't know much about the issues or whether they follow through on what they promise. All they know about is whether they feel good about the President's personality.

These paragraphs actually contain a number of concepts and variables, a network of relationships, and a whole series of hypotheses. But at least there is some indication of the possibilities for a more focused study.

At this point two levels of study could be mounted: *descriptive* and *relational*. A *descriptive study* collects information about a situation. One might describe an institution, event, or behavior, or some combination of these. Good description is the beginning of science. Leonardo da Vinci's masterful notes and drawings of human anatomy enabled generations of medical scientists to advance their understanding of the body. Some specialized descriptive studies analyze information about a single variable—for example, the breakdown of families. What does it consist of? How much of it is going on? When does it occur most frequently? These studies are valuable sources for higher forms of analysis.

Relational analysis examines connections between things. The basic form consists of probing the links between one variable and another: the relation between education and voting, for example, or between intelligence and financial success. A series of relational studies can form the basis for causal analysis, that special type of relational study in which the most powerful of connections between variables is isolated.

The initial thoughts on the topic given in the preceding paragraphs seem to imply a whole series of relations. If you are impatient to get to the root of the situation, a relational analysis of some aspect of the general problem of democratic accountability might be most satisfying.

Hypothesis Formation

With the topic narrowed somewhat, hypothesis formation becomes easier. The question is twofold: What are the essential variables? What are the relations between them? One intriguing element of our sample problem involves two variables: *assessments of candidates* and *voting behavior*. The paragraphs that were written suggest a link between the two. What is the nature of the link? What word expresses that relationship? If we leave aside causal analysis, the suggested relationship is a simple one: People are more likely to vote for candidates with charismatic personalities.

Even with all these words, we still have only two variables and one relationship: *candidate perception* ASSOCIATED WITH *voting decision*. Most studies, of course, contain several hypotheses, possibly interconnected as elements of one large thesis. But for purposes of illustration we will stay with something less demanding.

Operationalizing Concepts

To operationalize a concept means to put it in a form that permits some kind of measurement of variation. As discussed in Chapter 2, operationalization turns concepts into usable variables. Translating a concept into something that allows the observation of variation is a tricky process. If it is done properly, two conditions will be met: (1) the operational version will fit the meaning of the original concept as closely as possible (*validity*); (2) the measurement(s) of variation can be replicated by others (*reliability*).

How does one operationalize voter assessments of candidates? Well, how about asking a simple question:

> *What is it about candidate X that would make you vote for her/him?*

Once the answer is given to this question, it then becomes a matter of identifying patterns in the responses. We can look at the responses and see if any themes emerge. The most frequently mentioned themes should give us a clue as to how voters make up their minds.

The variation in *voter assessments of candidates* has to do with perceived candidate characteristics. The variation in these assessments can be captured in categories of responses. If people say they would vote for Bill Clinton because he is handsome, rather than because he is experienced in making executive decisions, then we know something about what shapes those individuals' *voting decision.*

Looking back at the preceding two paragraphs, the main hypothesis is about the importance of personal characteristics such as appearance or charisma relative to other traits such as integrity, competence, and reliability. Normative theories of democracy suggest that voters in a well-functioning polity would select leaders on the basis of their likely performance rather than on superficial, personal qualities such as physical appearance. Classical democratic theories also contend that education should facilitate a well-functioning democracy by equipping the average person with the ability to judge effectively the competence of candidates for public office. It would be interesting to see if these categories of responses show up in studies of how voters assess candidates, and, if they do, which characteristics appear to be most influential.

At this point, we will observe the strategy actually used in a study by Arthur Miller, Martin Wattenberg, and Oksana Malanchuk entitled, "Schematic Assessments of Presidential Candidates."[2] A condensed version of the article is reprinted as Appendix A in this book. Read it over; this will enhance your understanding as we explore how the study was done. The study is an example of a well-constructed and carefully presented research project. The authors begin by discussing the theoretical background of their work, the steps taken in generating and testing hypotheses, and the larger meaning of their results. This is the model to follow—even for a brief research paper.

In operationalizing the variable *voter assessments of candidates,* the authors examined answers to the following questions asked in presidential election surveys from 1952 to 1984:

---

[2]In *American Political Science Review* 80, no. 2 (June 1986):521–540.

> *Is there anything in particular about the [Democratic/ Republican/Independent] candidate that might make you want to vote for him?*
>
> *Is there anything in particular about the [Democratic/ Republican/Independent] candidate that might make you want to vote against him?*

The authors looked for patterns in the kinds of answers given. Five themes appeared with striking consistency:

Competence
Integrity
Reliability
Charisma
Personal characteristics

Voters frequently mentioned these considerations in explaining their positive—and negative—assessments of presidential candidates. Furthermore, there was a high level of agreement among the different researchers who read the same responses that they fit into one or another of these five categories. Now, having operationalized the key variable voter assessments of candidates in terms of these five categories, the stage is set for organizing the whole inquiry.

Reality Testing

Organizing the Bibliography

With a hypothesis in mind, it is good idea to do some additional reading before actually beginning research. This will help you check your formulation of hypotheses and operationalization of variables against other efforts. Articles, books, and journal reports are all valuable sources for information and background. Often a single journal article on the topic will contain footnotes and bibliography that can guide you to most of the significant literature on the subject. A more sophisticated researcher would take this step first—it can save a lot of time in the thinking-it-over stage. However, beginning students often come to problems of social analysis "fresh."

Doing Research

Not many students could mount the kind of research effort suggested here. However, for instructional purposes, it is sufficient to see how an example of social science research works so that your own project can be formulated with the clearest possible strategy.

Arthur Miller and his associates tested their hypotheses by re-analyzing surveys that had already been done. A lot of social science is carried on in this way. As researchers look at "old" data with a different perspective, and a new hypothesis, fresh insights are revealed. In doing your own research, check with faculty members and the library to see if there might be data that could be used to test your hypotheses before you set out to collect your own.

In this case, the authors looked at presidential election studies from 1952 to 1984 to summarize the answers to the open-ended questions. They knew on the basis of prior research that voters mention their assessment of the candidates more often than party affiliation or issue positions in explaining why they vote as they do. However, Miller and his colleagues wanted to "get inside" the question of how candidates are assessed to see just what qualities seem to impress voters the most (or least).

Rather than deciding in advance what characteristics were most significant, they let the themes emerge from the summaries of answers that were given. For example, the following phrases were found in the kinds of answers grouped in the category of *competence:*

experienced
has good record in public service
a statesman
independent
no one runs him
well-informed
down-to-earth
makes a lot of sense

Voters who stressed *personal* considerations mentioned such qualities as:

health
age
appearance/looks on TV
wealth
morality

For the sample as whole, Miller and his associates counted the number of responses that fit into each of the five categories (*competence, integrity, reliability, charisma, personal characteristics*). For example, if someone commented on President Carter's ability to get the Mideast peace talks under way, that is tabulated as a *competence* response. If a voter in 1972 said that President Nixon did not keep his pledge to end the Vietnam War, and that this made it likely that he or she would vote against him, that is counted as an *integrity* response. The summary of the responses reveals some interesting patterns (see Table 3.1) and permits some interesting observations: for example, in assessing candidates, *voters are most influenced by competence.* As you can see, *competence* was the most important characteristic voters mentioned in every year of the survey. In 1984, 39 percent of the sample mentioned considerations that reflect on competence such as experience, being well informed, and "makes a lot of sense." The least important consideration in every election since 1960 seems to be *charisma*.

In any case, the results may seem to have provided a happy ending to the study, but there is more to concluding a study than simply saying: "See, I was right (or wrong)!"

Analyzing the Results

Results need to be placed in perspective. In this study, the real issue was whether such personal attributes as appearance or charisma are more important than substantive considerations such as competence, reliability, and integrity. It appears that the latter three constitute a majority of the responses (a total of 72 percent in 1984 versus 28 percent for charisma and personal attributes combined). Now, it may be that voters just don't want to admit that they like Ronald Reagan's smile or thought Jimmy Carter wasn't all that much fun to look at. One study seldom settles all the important issues. But is is interesting that personal characteristics are *less often* given in recent years than previously. With the increasing significance of media politics, we might think it would be the other way around.

Another analytic device is to see what impact other significant variables have on the results. Level of education might have

TABLE 3.1   VOTER ASSESSMENTS OF PRESIDENTIAL CANDIDATE CHARACTERISTICS, 1952–1984

Characteristic	1952	1956	1960	1964	1968	1972	1976	1980	1984
Competence	36%	41%	46%	39%	42%	42%	39%	44%	39%
Integrity	14	15	9	18	16	25	27	16	16
Reliability	5	5	8	24	19	22	13	16	17
Charisma	10	9	6	8	9	5	5	5	10
Personal	35	30	31	11	14	6	16	19	18

NOTE: Table entries are percentages of all comments from the five dimensions (categories).

SOURCE: National Election Studies, University of Michigan Center for Political Studies. The table is adapted from table in A. Miller et al., "Schematic Assessments of Presidential Candidates," *American Political Science Review* 80, no. 2 (June 1986), p. 529.

something to do with how people assess candidates. The data shown in Table 3.2 seem to bear that out. In this table, what is being counted is the average number of comments made about specific candidate characteristics by respondents in each education category. As we can see, college-educated respondents make more comments than people with less education—no surprise there! It is also notable that for all education levels, *competence* is at the top of the list and *charisma* is at the bottom. The biggest variation associated with level of education concerns *integrity* and *reliability.*

To conclude, we want to emphasize that by consulting other reality tests, you can gain perspective on the utility of the one you have constructed. At the same time, other studies can provide a general check on your findings.

Understanding the Results

Evaluating Concept Operationalization and Variable Measurement

Now that you have some research experience with the subject, rethink each step of the strategy in light of what happened. There is a big difference between thinking of a way to

TABLE 3.2   AVERAGE NUMBER OF COMMENTS ABOUT CANDIDATE CHARACTERISTICS BY LEVEL OF EDUCATION

Education	*Competence*	*Integrity*	*Reliability*	*Charisma*	*Personal*
Grade School	.58	.19	.19	.10	.37
High School	.76	.38	.29	.19	.47
College	1.15	.74	.66	.29	.48

NOTE: The numbers of comments per characteristic were averaged over the years 1952–1984.

SOURCE: National Election Studies, University of Michigan Center for Political Studies. The table is adapted from table in Miller et al., "Schematic Assessments . . . ," p. 531.

operationalize a concept and having it work as expected in the process of research.

Some questions for this project are:

1. Can you be sure that voters were thinking of a candidate's competence when they noted, for example, "he speaks with common sense"? (This was one of the responses included as a competence assessment.) Would it be more appropriate to categorize the statement as an assessment of personality?
2. Do the five categories represent schema that actually organize voters' thoughts, or are they abstractions created by the researchers' interpretation of the data?
3. Can the wide variety of responses to open-ended questions be boiled down to five distinct categories?
4. Did the open-ended question seem to get at each of the five categories of assessment?

We also need to consider how the survey data might be biased. There is the problem of a person's state of mind in answering a question. Any number of factors can influence responses. Liquor can't be sold in some states on election day so as to avoid muddling the judgment of voters. Beyond chemical disturbance is the possibility of other intervening events— for example, female interviewers might produce different responses from women than male interviewers do. It is useful to repeat studies in different times and places. If you ask college students to fill out questionnaires, be ready for the campus wit. The jokers, the devious, and the perverse can foul up a questionnaire in many ways.

Another possible form of interference with honest responses arises from respondents who feel there is something fishy about the project, the researcher, the questions, or the presumed confidentiality of the responses. An erstwhile sophomore once polled the faculty of a church-affiliated college about their personal use of marijuana. She did these interviews in person and assured the faculty that each response would be "confidential"—the data summaries were to be broken down by department and rank, and the final paper would then be placed in the library. However, a junior faculty member in a small department might conceivably have been wary of the promised confidentiality and been less than honest in responding to such an invitation to persecution if not prosecution.

In dealing with people, science does not substitute for savvy.

Were the Measures Any Good?

Self-criticism isn't a particularly welcome task, but in social science it serves two specific purposes. Obviously, it helps to re-examine a project after you've finished to be sure that the steps along the way are sufficiently well done to lead directly to the conclusion. Reexamination serves another function, however. In dealing with something as slippery as the measurement of social phenomena, whatever is learned in the development and use of measures needs to be shared. A measure can look very impressive at the outset of an inquiry. The experience gained in actually using it, however, may turn up some unexpected weaknesses that, if stated as part of the results, can save someone else a lot of work.

In the case of Miller et al.'s project, hundreds of verbal responses were analyzed. Five distinct, underlying factors were found to organize the responses.[3] The authors used a procedure known as *factor analysis* that reveals patterns in information. The next question was whether the patterns reflect some underlying themes, such as assessments of competence. Factor analysis reveals how many unique patterns exist

---

[3]Factor analysis is messy business. A discussion of how to do it is beyond the scope of this text. Interested readers can consult Jae-On Kim and Charles W. Mueller, *Introduction to Factor Analysis*, Sage University Paper Series on Quantitative Applications in Social Science no. 13 (Beverly Hills, Calif.: 1978); or William Dillon and Matthew Goldstein, *Multivariate Analysis* (New York: Wiley, 1984), ch. 3.

among the responses; however, it does not show what the patterns represent.

Remember that Miller et al. were trying to create a measure that captures variation in voters' assessments of candidates. They noted a pattern of responses that included comments such as "independent," "has a good record in public service," "down-to-earth," and "makes sense." They thought that these responses "involve the candidate's past political experience, ability as a statesman, comprehension of political issues" and decided to call it "competence."[4] Is it? The responses Miller and his colleagues used for measuring competence can be criticized for being too broadly defined. Perhaps some other theme is represented by the responses. Maybe "competence" is too general to have meaning as a distinct category in the voter's mind.

Does this criticism invalidate the measure? No; there is no such thing as a perfect measure. The point is to be able to defend your measure against likely alternatives. A researcher must have a good defense of how variables are measured and defined. In this example, Miller et al. decided to lump responses into distinct groups so that variation in assessments of candidates could be dealt with in five workable categories. Some researchers use measures of candidate assessments (or leadership qualities) that rely on forced-choice questions. In such an approach, the researcher defines the categories of candidate assessment ahead of time and asks respondents to choose among them.[5] Comparing findings ob-

---

[4]Miller et al., p. 528.

[5]For example, see Clive Bean and Anthony Mughan, "Leadership Effects in Parliamentary Elections in Australia and Britain," *American Political Science Review* 83, no. 4 (December 1989):1165–1180. These authors asked about the qualities party leaders possess, and respondents had to choose between the following: *caring, determined, shrewd, likable as a person, tough, listens to reason, decisive, sticks to principles, effective* (p. 1168).

tained by these different approaches to observation helps build understanding.

Can Statistics Be Trusted?

Assorted mystics throughout the ages have made much of examining the entrails of birds for portents and predictions of the future. Those skilled in statistical criticism are probably the modern heirs of this profession (particularly those who are adept at finding good news and bad news in any given statistic). That statistics do not provide, in and of themselves, precise answers to social inquiries surprises some and comforts others. It is easy to say that statistics can lie, or that they never quite get the whole message across and are therefore useless. But the question is: Statistics (or measurement) compared to what? Compared to language concepts such as "more," "less," "a whole bunch," or "a little bit," statistics can be more precise. It is true that evidence involving numbers can be misleading; but words can mislead too. Symbolic cues, loaded terms, imprecise language—all distort knowledge. The advantage of a scientific approach to observation is that biases can be more easily exposed because the specification of meanings and procedures is so explicit.

Of course, the wrong statistic can be used as easily as the wrong word, and science is no substitute for common sense. As you learn more about statistics, you will find that researchers typically use several statistics to summarize a situation, rather than relying on a single indicator in order to compensate for the faults of any particular statistic.

How Do Your Findings Fit with Theories in the Field?

Although a simple experiment or inquiry may answer some puzzle that is on your mind, it may also relate in interesting ways to more general issues that are contained within theories of the subject. For example, it is mildly interesting to know how education influences people's judgments of presidential candidates. It is a lot more interesting to fit that finding to a whole set of ideas about the human condition. Can we indeed be trusted to select our own leaders? Does democracy really work? These are large theoretical perspectives, but theory doesn't have to be grand to be good. There are less global theories that explain key pieces of events.

Miller and his colleagues begin and end their article by discussing democratic theory as well as previous research on the judgments voters make when selecting their leaders. They cite other writers who take a dim view of voting on the basis of candidate personality. In these cases, personality assessments were seen as superficial and not in the best interests of a democratic society. Taken to an extreme, such behavior might continually produce slickly packaged, attractive candidates who make incompetent leaders. This discussion highlights the relevance of Miller et al.'s study. They show that voters are searching for a deeper analysis, which other studies neglected to identify. Many voters do evaluate candidates on the basis of their personality, but it isn't just charm that is considered. Voters use personality traits as clues to competence and integrity.[6] Thus, the rise of candidate-centered, personality politics in America does not necessarily reflect superficial evaluations on the part of voters.

In evaluating this study, refer to the general readings you have done. Also, if time allows, do some more investigations of

---

[6]Empirical research on human development indicates that *competence* and *integrity* are what people aspire to in forming their own identities. An interesting theoretical connection can be made here between social psychology and democratic theory. Cf. Erik Erikson, *Childhood and Society,* 2d ed. rev. (New York: Norton, 1963 [1st ed., 1950]), pp. 240, 268–269; Kenneth Hoover, "Identity and Democratization," presented at the World Congress of the International Political Science Association, Berlin, August 1994.

what other people have found out about voters' perceptions of candidates. Think about how democracy could be strengthened by making better information available about the competence and integrity of politicians.

A noteworthy scientist once commented that "science is observation," by which he meant to suggest that getting all wound up in the details of experimental and control groups, statistics, and the rest can obscure the purpose of scientific inquiry: using your head to understand what is going on.[7] There is no such thing as the perfect experiment that explains everything about a given phenomenon. Be wary of people who say they have proven something—especially with "facts" based on statistics. Use the scientific method as a critical tool as well as a means of discovery. Seek out vulnerable assumptions and the limitations of evidence so that you know both what has been demonstrated and what has not.[8]

Scientific procedure is lifeless by itself. In the hands of an imaginative researcher it becomes a very useful tool, but the mind is a far more subtle instrument than any set of procedures for investigation. Where science as method ends, scientists as *people* take over.

In relating your work to theory and in speculating about its larger consequences, you have a chance to be imaginative and creative, though not undisciplined or completely fanciful. Charles Fourier, a French socialist, extended the observation that people work better and are happier in communes to the notion that advances in human understanding would cause world history to ascend (through hundreds of years) to a situa-

---

[7]Robert Hodes, "Aims and Methods of Scientific Research," Occasional Paper no. 9 (New York: American Institute of Marxist Studies, 1968), pp. 11–14.

[8]For examples of questionable uses of science, see Daisie Radner and Michael Radner, *Science and Unreason* (Belmont, Calif.: Wadsworth, 1982).

tion so utopian that every day would begin with a parade, the oceans would turn into lemonade, and we would be transported across the seas by friendly whales. That's a bit much.

CONCEPTS INTRODUCED

Fact	Descriptive study
Truth	Relational analysis
Falsifiable statements	Operationalization

QUESTIONS FOR DISCUSSION

1. One version of "reality testing" in science involves comparing some observed relationship to how the results would appear if no relationship existed between variables. Look at Table 3.2 in this chapter: What would the data look like if there were no relationship between education and assessments of candidates?

2. After reading the Miller et al. article in Appendix A, examine the section at the end, where the authors list the responses that fit into the five categories of the variable *candidate assessment*. This is how the authors operationalize the variable. Might some of the responses reflect another, unidentified category of assessment?

3. Can you think of other ways of operationalizing voters' assessments of candidates in order to understand the role of personality in politics?

4. Do you think that respondents might give socially acceptable reasons in justifying their voting decisions—justifications that conceal their real motives? Is there any way to design a study that would avoid this problem of validity?

OUTLINE

CHAPTER FOUR

REFINEMENTS

"Enthusiasm and deep conviction are necessary if men and women are to explore all the possibilities of any new idea, and later experience can be relied on either to confirm or to moderate the initial claims—for science flourishes on a double programme of speculative liberty and unsparing criticism."

STEPHEN TOULMIN AND
JUNE GOODFIELD

Developing a sense for the methodology of social science resembles learning to play pool. The basic elements of each are simple—in pool: a table, some balls, and a stick; in social science: variables, measurements, and hypotheses. Up to now, we have been looking at the simple shots: a hypothesis with two fairly obvious variables and a measurement of the relations between them. In science, as in pool, the more elaborate strategies are variations on the basic technique. A good pool player never tries a harder shot than absolutely necessary; so also with a social scientist. Likewise, professionals in both fields have had to invent techniques for minimizing error and getting around obstacles. In this chapter and the next, we will discuss the elements in

67

a slightly different order from previous chapters—hypotheses, variables, and then measurements—and explore some refinements of each. In other words, we will illustrate some bank shots in the corner pocket.

Hypotheses

Hypotheses do not spring full-blown from the intellect unencumbered by a web of thoughts and preferences. Like any other artifact of human behavior, a hypothesis is part of a mosaic of intentions, learnings, and concerns. Social scientists have debated long and hard over how to deal with this reality. Some have preferred that the researcher do everything possible to forget values and other biases in order to concentrate on "objectively" pursuing work in the name of professional social science. Others have insisted that ignoring the origins of a hypothesis is inefficient because it leads the researcher to ignore basic factors in his or her own approach to data.

There is another whole set of questions related to how hypotheses fit with such structures of thought as theories, models, or, to use a more recent word, paradigms. The formation of useful theories is, after all, the end object of the exercise. Thus, the relations between theory and research require exploration.

Finally, there is the somewhat more mundane, operational matter of the kinds of relationships that can be built into hypotheses. These three topics—the roles of values, theories, and relationships in the formation of hypotheses—will be dealt with consecutively.

Values and Hypothesis Formation

The notion of values is in itself peculiar. Writers have often tried to come to grips with what a value is and how one value can be separated from another. The sticky part is that values are hard to isolate. I may believe in freedom, but not freedom to the exclusion of equality, or freedom for certain kinds of behavior, such as theft. Values occur in webs of mutually modifying conditions. The confused self we all experience often may be seen acting out different sets of values at different moments, with a larger pattern visible only over a substantial time period. Still there remains a kind of consistency to human character— enough so that we can and do make general estimates of the orientation to life that people have.

Social scientists generally have resolved the problem of the relation of values to research by recommending that one's value orientations be discussed in presenting a report of a project. Because values are such an intimate part of every step of forming a hypothesis, selecting measures, and evaluating conclusions, that is a fair request. However, the specification cannot be an afterthought. The role of values has to be squarely faced at the outset of inquiry. Unless that is done, you may not see what your values are doing to your research. For example, someone who is strongly religious might do research on dating habits involving questions that are premised on the immorality of premarital intercourse. The questions used might easily reflect such a bias and invite respondents to condemn a practice that they in fact approve.

Of Theories, Models, and Paradigms

The relationship of a hypothesis, or an inquiry, to theories and models of phenomena seems commonsensical but becomes steadily more complicated when authors try to set down the relationship in writing. We know what a theory is—a set of related propositions that attempts to explain, and sometimes to predict, a set of events. By now we also know what a hypothesis is. In a rough sense, a theory is a collection of hypotheses linked by some kind of logical framework. The term "theory" connotes a degree of uncertainty about whether the understanding it offers is valid and correct. Theories, then, are tentative formulations. That which has been demonstrated to defy falsification usually is embodied in sets of "laws" or axioms.

Two other terms enter into the discussion. Scientists use the term "model" to convey an implication of greater order and system in a theory. Models represent simplifications of reality in a manner that allows examination of key relationships. Economists, for instance, are heavily involved in efforts to create theoretical models in which unemployment, inflation, and other major variables associated with economic performance are related mathematically.

On the other hand, the term "paradigm" (which comes from a Latin root meaning "pattern") refers to a larger frame of understanding, shared by a wider community of scientists, that organizes smaller-scale theories and inquiries. For generations in antiquity, astronomy was dominated by a paradigm that placed earth at the center of the universe. Early observers of the heavens tried to explain all other stellar phenomena within that context; ultimately, of course, the paradigm collapsed with the advent of a much more powerful explanation.

There are few laws and axioms in social science, some vague paradigms, a good many theories, and lately some intriguing models. For those at the beginning of social scientific investigation, theory is best conceived of as a guide to inquiry—a way of organizing and economizing insight so as to avoid the trivial and isolate the significant.

In social science there are two general modes by which theory comes into play: inductive and deductive. *Induction* refers to building theory through the accumulation and summation of a variety of inquiries. *Deduction* has to do with using the logic of a theory to generate propositions that can then be tested.

The most popular image of science has researchers collecting bits of information through a gradual process of investigation and forming them into theories. The test then becomes whether or not the theory explains what is known about a phenomenon. The danger in accepting the simple view of science as induction

*"Dynamite, Mr. Gerston! You're the first person I ever
heard use 'paradigm' in real life."*

Drawing by Lorenz; © 1974 The New Yorker Magazine, Inc.

is that the categories used in constructing the inquiry may reflect
an implicit theory. What is presented as induction turns out to be
a hidden form of deduction. Scientific procedure is designed to
reduce such biases by requiring that the propositions in a theory
to be put in falsifiable form: that is, that they be subject to
testing. As clear as that requirement would seem to be, social
investigation is so value-laden and the tools for reality testing so
limited that mistaken judgments can easily be made.

Deduction is becoming an increasingly common way of
relating theory to research. Under pressure of attack from critics of the supposedly "objective" nature of social science, researchers are beginning to understand that deduction subtly

enters into the formation of basic concepts commonly used in hypotheses. In American culture, the pervasive conditioning to a capitalist political-economic system has led many political scientists, sociologists, and economists to take our system as the norm of the good society and to cast all nonmarket patterns of behavior into such negative categories as deviant, counter-productive, underdeveloped, and so on. The connotations of these labels are, in a real sense, deduced from a larger theory that implies the naturalness or rightness of one system of political economy. Yet these labels are presented as inductively determined "scientific" designations.[1]

Proceeding from such culture-bound assumptions, it becomes easier to argue that an individual who acts on motives other than material self-interest is "poorly adjusted or "irrational" or in need of treatment or confinement. In fact, what is labeled as irrational behavior may serve needs repressed in a capitalist society and therefore may help one adapt to a difficult environment—as, for instance, in the behavior of the poor person who buys a fancy car. Owning a car may be the one way for the person to give the appearance of success, to regard himself or herself as someone of consequence, and to attract attention from an otherwise uncaring world. That the payments deplete the food budget may strike the middle-class observer as foolish largely because middle-class observers, those with jobs at any rate, do not suffer the stress of constant rejection and personal humiliation.

Since deduction is a natural pattern of thought, it needs to be harnessed to scientific exploration. Very often deductions from theory provide the basic agenda of a field of inquiry. Established theories are guides to the solutions of many particular puzzles. The deductive "route" is well worth trying before starting anew in the task of explanation.

---

[1]See Murray Edelman, *Political Languages: Words That Succeed and Policies That Fail* (New York: Academic Press, 1977).

There is no need to carry this navel-gazing about induction and deduction too far. A good scientific inquiry always contains elements that make it possible for others who have differing perspectives to judge its worth. The principal reason to keep these points in mind is to be conscious of self-delusion and of the ways others are misleading in their presentation of scientific findings.

Long before you are able to deal with the formation of theories, you will be a consumer of theory retailed by others. In utilizing research results, a precautionary question needs to be asked about the theory in terms of which the results are conceived to be meaningful. It is similar to the question about the values behind an inquiry, and it consists of understanding the theoretical perspective from which an inquiry is undertaken. Never read a social science work without paying careful attention to the introduction and preface—therein usually lies the key to the author's commitments.

At the same time, do not be afraid to play with theoretical explanation as a guide to your own efforts. Science is very democratic, and anyone can take an investigative pot shot at a theory or try to extend it in new ways. By becoming aware of the predominant theories in a field, you can save some of your own time by borrowing their vision to see what the possible explanations of a phenomenon are.

Relationships in Hypotheses

Independent and Dependent Variables Not all variables are equal. If social science only managed to show that prejudice is associated with ignorance, youth with rebellion, and IQ with breast-feeding, social scientists wouldn't have done as much as the culture has a right to expect. Are people prejudiced because they are ignorant, or ignorant because they wear the blinders of prejudice? Which precedes the other? We almost said, which *causes* the other, but did not because conclusive

73

demonstrations of causation require elaborate procedures. The notion of independence and dependence in variables is a way of sneaking up on the question of causation without trying to go the whole distance.

An *independent* variable is one that influences another variable, called the *dependent* variable. For example, as heat increases, air can hold more water. Heat is an independent variable; the amount of water that can be suspended in the air, a dependent variable. What happens to the water *depends on* changes in temperature. If the air is soggy with moisture and heat goes down, water starts falling out of the air—which even social scientists refer to as rain.

In the example on education and voter assessments of candidates presented in Chapter Three, Miller et al. suggested that *education* is the independent variable and *assessment of candidates* the dependent variable. The ability to assess candidates in terms of abstract qualities such as "competence" might well be associated with a college education. Thus, the hypothesis is that the ability to assess candidates in abstract terms is influenced by (or depends upon) education. It is hard to think this might work the other way around; how could *assessment of candidates* influence *education*? Reversing the relationship is a good way of seeing whether a presumed relationship of dependence makes sense.

There's nothing very tricky about the notion of independence and dependence. But there is something tricky about the fact that the relationship of independence and dependence is a figment of the researcher's imagination until demonstrated convincingly. Researchers *hypothesize* relationships of independence and dependence: they invent them, and then they try by observation and analysis to see if the relationships actually work out that way.

The question of independent and dependent variables can be more clearly understood when seen in the form social scientists are fondest of—tables. Tables are a method of presenting data, but behind a table is often a hypothesis that escapes the attention of the novice.

Consider Table 4.1. Which is the independent variable? Which the dependent variable? How would you reconstruct the hypothesis that these data support?

The two variables are *race* and *political activity*. What do the data say about the relationship between these two variables? The answer is that whites have been slightly more involved than blacks in some kinds of political activities. Race influences participation. Therefore, race is the presumed independent variable and participation is the dependent variable. To check on the assignment of the labels "independent" and "dependent," reverse the hypothesis. Could the level of political activity influence what race a person is? No.

Table 4.1 illustrates the form in which tables are usually presented. The independent variable is listed across the *top* and the dependent variable down the *side*. By presenting tables in this standard fashion, researchers can locate the relationship without having to think about it. Nevertheless, it is a very good practice when looking at a table to formulate the hypotheses it is supposed to test. The author may have reversed the

TABLE 4.1   POLITICAL ACTIVITY AMONG BLACKS AND
WHITES

	Blacks	*Whites*
Worked for a party or a candidate[a]	4%	5%
Attended a political meeting or rally[a]	7	8
Contributed money to a party or candidate[a]	4	10
Attended a public meeting on a local issue[b]	12	18
Wrote a letter to a congressman/senator[b]	5	16
Voted	53	68

[a]Averaged from data from National Election Studies, 1952–1988.
[b]Averaged from data from Roper Surveys, 1976–1988, Roper Starch Worldwide, Inc.

SOURCE: Adapted from Steven J. Rosenstone and John Mark Hansen, *Mobilization, Participation and Democracy in America* (New York: Macmillan, 1993), 44.

usual location of the independent and dependent variables for reasons of emphasis, style, or convenience.

Alternative, Antecedent, and Intervening Variables One of the central problems in developing strong hypotheses lies in understanding how variables stand in relation to each other. In hypothesizing connections between variables, you need to be aware of variables other than the ones you have selected that may be involved in producing changes in a relationship. Social scientists commonly refer to *alternative, antecedent,* and *intervening variables.*

All three terms have commonsense meanings. An alternative variable is an additional independent variable that influences changes in the dependent variable. An antecedent is something that comes before. For example, the antecedent of birth is conception. To intervene means to come between. We will illustrate each of these concepts more precisely.

If one considers the variables that influence whether or not a person votes, several appear: attitudes toward government, the difficulty of registration procedures, the weather on election day, the person's level of information about politics, and so on. These are alternative variables. To establish the link between race and voting participation (see Table 4.1) is useful nonetheless, though a complete account of why people do or do not vote would have to include the influence of all the significant alternative variables. Race does influence participation, but education and other variables intervene. If important variables are left out, the results may be meaningless or—as social scientists like to say—*spurious.* We shall return to the issue of spuriousness in the next chapter.

Another classic illustration of an antecedent variable comes from the history of research on voting behavior. It became obvious from early surveys that more highly educated people tend to vote Republican. From that relationship, it could be implied that well-educated people are politically conservative. However, it turns out that there is a powerful antecedent variable that influences both the *level of education* and *voting behavior: parental wealth.* In fact, those who are highly educated tend to come from wealthier families, and wealthier families are more likely to vote Republican. What was being measured in the correlation of *education* with *voting behavior* was really the prior influence of *parental wealth* on the political preferences of their children.

As for intervening variables, suppose you are told that Hollygood Bread has fewer calories per slice than six other brands. The advertising leads you to assume that the independent variable is Hollygood's special formula for low-calorie dough. But you come to find out that the real reason for the difference is that the Hollygood company slices its bread thinner than the others. The dough actually has about as many calories as Sunshaft Bread or even Wondergoo. The thinness of the slice is the intervening variable between quality of dough and calories per slice.

To use a more elegant example, consider the relationship between education and social status. These two variables are positively associated; however, everyone knows of people who have modest educations but high social status. The reason might be that another variable enters the picture: occupational success.

To see how occupational success intervenes between education and status, think of the people you know who are poorly educated but who enjoy average status by virtue of their success at their job (group A). Now think of those who are well educated, successful, and high in status (group B). Think of yet a third group who are well educated but who have had lousy luck in the job market and have middling status by conventional standards (group C).

If you worked only with the relationship between education and status or that between occupation and status, rather than with all three variables, you would miss the point of the relationship between either pair. Group A would have you thinking that there is little connection between education and status, yet group B would make it appear that status and education go together like peanut butter and jelly. Meanwhile group C, just as educated as group B, has only average status. The same confusion would result from considering only the relationship between occupational success and status.

In general, well-educated people (group B) have higher status than poorly educated folks (group A). Thus, it is demonstrable that education contributes to success. However, occupational success intervenes between education and conventional social status.

The way to avoid getting trapped by alternative, antecedent, and intervening variables is to do some thinking before formulating a hypothesis. Take the dependent variable and ask yourself what all the possible independent variables might be. If you want to explain why some people are fatalistic, think of all the variables that could influence such a state of mind. Possibilities might include the nature of their work, money troubles, unrequited love, background characteristics, the weather, or peer-group influences. In fact, most social phenomena—perhaps *all* social phenomena—are influenced by several variables. The point of worrying about alternative, antecedent, and intervening variables is not so much to discourage investigation of what interests you as to put it into perspective so that you do not confuse association with causation.

As another example, consider the argument frequently heard during election campaigns over the effect of state taxes on the employment rate. Critics of the cost of government are heard to argue that lowering taxes will stimulate the state's economy by attracting businesses that don't like to pay taxes, thus adding new jobs and reducing unemployment. In Figure 4.1, we have indicated some of the antecedent, intervening, and alternative variables that might have an impact on a state's unemployment rate.

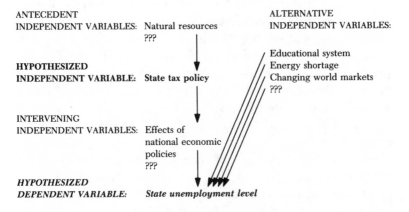

POSSIBLE INDEPENDENT VARIABLES

ANTECEDENT
INDEPENDENT VARIABLES: Natural resources
???

HYPOTHESIZED
INDEPENDENT VARIABLE: State tax policy

INTERVENING
INDEPENDENT VARIABLES: Effects of
national economic
policies
???

HYPOTHESIZED
DEPENDENT VARIABLE: **State unemployment level**

ALTERNATIVE
INDEPENDENT VARIABLES:

Educational system
Energy shortage
Changing world markets
???

A careful sorting out reveals that there are many independent variables involved, any one of which is likely to be more significant than the one hypothesized: state tax policy. In fact, higher state taxes, insofar as they affect the educational system, may be the key to improving employment rather than the reverse.[2]

Once you recognize the variables that have a significant influence on a dependent variable, there are ways of separating out the influence of one variable from another. The simplest technique is to "control" for one variable by holding it constant, while two others are tested for their relationship to each other. In the example of the connections between parental wealth,

[2]See, for example, Bryan D. Jones, "Public Policies and Economic Growth in the American States," *Journal of Politics,* 52 (1990):219–234. Jones finds that the overall size of the public sector is not associated with economic decline and that spending on education, highways, police, and fire protection is associated with employment gains and economic growth.

education, and voting behavior, one could select a sample of respondents with various levels of education from families of different wealth characteristics. If it turns out that highly educated children of wealthy families are predominantly Republicans, and that highly educated children of poorer families are predominantly Democrats, you know that education is far less powerful than family wealth in shaping voting behavior. Tables 4.2 and 4.3 illustrate this result.

As your methodological experience and sophistication increase, you will discover a host of techniques by which these connections can be sorted out. The first step in approaching the problem of sorting out variables is to understand the different levels of relationships that are built into hypotheses.

Levels of Relationships in Hypotheses The most distinctive characteristic of a hypothesis as opposed to most ordinary sentences is the care with which each term is specified. We

TABLE 4.2 EDUCATION AND PARTY IDENTIFICATION

Party Identification	Low Education	High Education	Total
Democrats	150	50	200
Republicans	50	150	200
Total	200	200	400

SOURCE: Simulated.

TABLE 4.3 EDUCATION AND PARTY IDENTIFICATION CONTROLLING FOR WEALTH

| Party Identification | From Poor Families | | | From Wealthy Families | | |
	Low Education	High Education	Total	Low Education	High Education	Total
Democrats	100	45	145	50	5	55
Republicans	5	10	15	45	140	185
Subtotal			160			240

SOURCE: Simulated.

have seen that the selection of variables is a serious task in itself. So also with the relationships that are specified between variables. In order to stretch your imagination a little, it is worth considering systematically the possible relationships that can be expressed between two or more variables. They comprise a spectrum, and we will discuss briefly each of the relationships presented in Table 4.4.

The null hypothesis is a rather ingenious creation. Remembering always that hypotheses are imagined relationships that are then put to the test, there is something to say for positing no relationship and then testing to see if the null hypothesis can be disproved, that is, if it can be demonstrated that some relationship does indeed exist.

The utility of the null hypothesis is that the case is not prejudged—you are not caught defending a relationship specified beforehand. In addition to withholding commitment to a specific relationship, you are also leaving open the possibility that one of the more substantial relationships may characterize the connection between the variables. It may be that there is an inferential or a correlative relationship that will emerge from the reality test. There may even be a direct or an inverse relationship, but those possibilities are left to emerge from the test itself.

TABLE 4.4   TYPES OF RELATIONSHIPS BETWEEN VARIABLES

Relationship	*Meaning*
Null	No relationship is presumed to exist.
Inferential/ Correlative	A relationship is presumed, but it is a relationship that deals with degrees of influence of one variable on another.
Direct/ Inverse	A specific correlative relationship is presumed in which one variable has a predictable association with another—either one variable increases as the other increases (direct) or one increases while the other decreases (inverse).
Causal	Changes in one variable are presumed to result from variations in another.

The null hypothesis is admirably suited to a cautious strategy of social investigation. A null hypothesis can be disproven simply by demonstrating that there is *any* sort of association between two variables. Causation requires an enormous burden of proof and is at the opposite end of the relationship spectrum from the null hypothesis.

Inferential and correlative relationships can be tested as a preliminary to moving in on causative relationships. The lesser relationships, interesting in themselves, are also screening devices. If, in the example of the relationship between education and voter assessments of candidates, a correlation that is statistically significant can be demonstrated, then there is some reason to press ahead with the work of separating out extraneous sources of error that may be responsible for the correlation. That done, the alternative sources of causation may be tested to see if a causal hypothesis might be justified.

Several things need to be understood about the relationship of causation. First, it is probably the end object of social science to decide what causes what. Therefore, there is tremendous interest in establishing causality. Second, it is the most difficult relationship to deal with because it demands the highest burden of proof. To prove that A causes B, you need to demonstrate that:

1. *A happens before B.* Obvious, isn't it?

2. *The occurrence of A is connected with the occurrence of B.* Obvious as well, but the connections of events are not always simple to discover. Some historians, for example, find a consistent link between the diets of reformers in the Middle Ages and the elaborateness of their visions. Joan of Arc, it is claimed, ate the wrong things, fouled up her digestive system, and so became a visionary and temporary heroine!

3. *A causes B; there isn't some other variable (C) that eliminates the variation in B associated with A.* This is where the going gets tough. It is always hard to eliminate all the possible influences, save one, in a situation. The time-honored

technique in experimental social science is to select two groups of subjects, duplicate as closely as possible everything in the environments of the two groups, and introduce the suspected causal variable to one group (the experimental group) and not to the other (the control group).

A classic example of the problems that arise in using the experimental-control group technique is the "Hawthorne" experiments, wherein one group of workers, the experimental group, was placed in a more pleasing physical environment for their assembly-line work. This experimental group consistently outproduced the control group, those working in the usual factory conditions. The trouble is that the increased productivity was later discovered to be mostly the effect of another variable—the special attention given the experimental group by the managers and experimenters themselves—rather than the physical surroundings. The experimenter had unknowingly introduced uncontrolled psychological factors: the two groups were differentiated by more than physical decor, thus violating the experimental-control group procedure and invalidating the results.

Most social scientists view the understanding of causation as the culmination of a long process of hypothesis formation and testing. The usual technique is to begin with a series of experiments to isolate the one variable that has the most obvious connection to the caused event. By this means, suspected sources of causation can be identified. The remaining logical steps usually demand a very high order of experimental elaboration. Consequently, beginners in the field are better off staying with relationships that can be more easily managed.

Because social science involves issues of great personal importance, it is hard to cultivate the habit of caution in hypothesis formation. Most beginners overstate their hypotheses, which leads them into measurement difficulties and the disappointments of an overworked conclusion. In trying to decide how strong a relationship to test for, give some thought to the measurements available as well as to the data resources within reach. A completely reported research experiment always contains the researcher's speculations about the larger ramifications of the results. But these are more palatable if the study itself observes sensible limits of hypothesis statement and measurement technique.

Establishing the logical relationships between variables in a hypothesis is, of course, a separate matter from testing to see if those relationships hold up. To see if a hypothesized relationship actually is borne out by observation, we need to move to the techniques of operationalization and measurement.

Variables

Operationalizing Concepts

Early in our discussion of social scientific concepts, we saw how language begins with the problem of assigning names to different phenomena. Social scientific language consists of agreements between people that a given behavior is properly referred to by a given name. To operationalize a variable means essentially to fit the name used for a behavior to some specific way of observing and measuring that behavior. Variable operationalizing, in a way, reverses the process by which language is formed: start with the name of the phenomenon that interests you, and work backward to find ways of tying that name to the specific behavior to which it refers.

The word "operationalization" makes the process discussed here sound special and expert, when in fact it is commonplace in everyday life. Late one evening, one of the authors of this book heard an argument in a saloon over which people are better, Kentuckians or West Virginians. The "discussion" revolved around such items as the observation that one person's cousin's uncle's father-in-law was from Kentucky and he was no damn good. However, by comparision, it seems that the other person's former boss married a woman whose nephew was from West Virginia and he was born to be hanged! After several volleys of this sort, it became clear that the variable, the quality of *Kentuckians* and *West Virginians,* had been operationalized in terms of the affinity for criminal behavior of people living in those states.

As any science develops, the number of variable names that refer to carefully specified objects, events, or behaviors increases. There are now in the social sciences whole catalogues of variables operationalized in terms of specific behaviors and possible measurements.[3]

With a little luck the variables that interest you have already been operationalized in a variety of ways. Even so, you need to know a number of techniques for operationalization in order to gain analytical flexibility and to be critical of what other people have done. In addition, you need to learn how to get around problems that arise when variables require forms of measurement that are outside your resources.

There are two ways of dealing with a variable that, for some reason, is not amenable to operationalization: *substitution* and *division.*

Suppose your hypothesis is this: *The more educated people are, the more likely they are to be socialists.* Education isn't hard to operationalize: the number of years spent in school tells you about exposure to formal education.

Whether people are socialists, and if so, how socialistic they are, is quite another matter. The ideology called socialism

[3]See John P. Robinson, Jerrold G. Rusk, and Kendra B. Head, *Measures of Political Attitudes* (1968); John P. Robinson, Robert Athanasiou, and Kendra B. Head, *Measures of Occupational Attitudes and Occupational Characteristics* (1969); John P. Robinson and Phillip R. Shaver, *Measures of Social Psychological Attitudes,* rev. ed. (1973); and Ki-Taek Chun, *Measures for Psychological Assessment* (1976). All are published by the Institute for Social Research of the University of Michigan, Ann Arbor.

brings together a complex of theories, versions of history, plans for action, and standards of good and bad. This bundle of things becomes all the harder to understand when it is realized that scholars of the subject have trouble agreeing on just what socialism means. Added to the difficulty of isolating a standard definition of socialism is the problem of dealing with unshared interpretations of the word on the part of the researcher, who is presumably trained in the formal ideological concept, and the sample survey respondent, who may think socialists are people who favor fluoridated water.

So it won't do to ask people, "Are you a socialist and, if so, how much of a socialist?" The answers to that question would generate some interesting data on self-perception, but the question would be too sloppy as a means of relating the respondents' attitudes to something as elaborate as socialist philosophy. *Substituting* for the variable *socialism* might solve some of those problems. Another variable could be found that pins down the attitudes involved more directly and deals with them in concrete terms. How about: *The more educated people become, the more they favor worker participation in management.*

The advantage here is that questions can be asked on a matter most people have an opinion about, and in terms that they can relate to. It does provide information relevant to the general hypothesis by picking up on an important element of socialist ideology even though it is a substitution.

Division is another way of dealing with a difficult variable. Behavior is very seldom simple; it occurs in the context of related actions, attitudes, and dispositions. Often the variables social scientists deal with can be seen as combinations of behavioral ingredients. The variable *alienation,* for example, may be divided into four specific characteristics that are tied to the way people are thought to feel when they are alienated: normless, powerless, meaningless, and helpless. Attitude scales have been developed to try to measure each of those attitude ingredients of alienation. By combining measures of all four attitudes or feelings, you will have data that could respectably be said to have something to do with alienation.

Dimensions of Variables

Variables often have different dimensions. A psychologist measuring personality might come up with a classification of introverted and extroverted personalities. He or she might also come up with a characterization of aggressivity-passivity on a scale from 1 to 10. These represent different dimensions of one variable: *personality.*

Public opinion usually is analyzed in terms of a variety of dimensions:

Direction: The *for*-ness or *against*-ness of the opinion.
Location: Where on the scale from *for* to *against* is the opinion found?
Intensity: How strongly or weakly held is the opinion?
Stability: How changeable is it?
Latency: How close to the surface of the opinion structure is it?
Salience: How important is that opinion in relation to others the person holds?[4]

All these dimensions contain different measurement possibilities, and there are a variety of techniques available to handle

---

[4]Adapted from Bradlee Karan, "Public Opinion and the New Ohio Criminal Code," The College of Wooster, Symposium on Public Opinion and the New Ohio Criminal Code, July 9–30, 1973, pp. 6–8; and Vladimir Orlando Key, Jr., *Public Opinion and American Democracy* (New York: Knopf, 1961), pp. 11–18.

Key discusses variables in terms of their *properties* rather than their *dimensions.* With respect to public opinion, he uses the term "dimension" where we have used "location." In recent usage, the term "properties" has become a general name for all the characteristics of a variable: its measurements as well as its various substantive components, or dimensions, which have acquired the more specific meaning to which we refer.

them. The *direction* of opinion requires only a specification that tells whether the opinion is on the "yes" side or the "no" side. *Salience,* on the other hand, allows an ordering of opinions from no salience to very great salience. *Intensity* of opinion suggests the possibility of scaling.

Before doing much work on a variable, think over which dimension you are looking at and what the other possible dimensions might be. Select those dimensions that are most promising in getting to the core of the variable. By looking at alternative dimensions, you can make choices as to which dimensions get to the crux of the variable and which dimensions can be measured by the means available to you. At the same time, understanding the different dimensions of a variable provides perspective on what has or has not yet been done to understand the variable.

One of the most persistant myths about science is that it can be entirely equated with measurement. As the foregoing chapter has tried to make clear, the real creativity in science goes into the operationalization of variables and the design of hypotheses. These very often require genuine creativity. Although measurement occasionally approaches an art form, it is more typically a matter of technique and the systematic application of mathematical concepts. As we shall see in the next chapter, measurement has its own logic and clever devices.

CONCEPTS INTRODUCED

Values	Deduction
Models	Independent variable
Paradigms	Dependent variable
Laws	Alternative variable
Axioms	Antecedent variable
Induction	Intervening variable

Refinements

Null hypothesis
Inferential relationship
Correlative relationship
Direct relationship
Inverse relationship

Causal relationship
Variable substitution
Variable division
Dimensions of variables

QUESTIONS FOR DISCUSSION

NOTE: Examine the data represented in Table 4.2 and Table 4.3. In this example, Table 4.2 is said to examine the relationship between education and party identification. In Table 4.3, party identification for people from both poor and wealthy families is examined. Table 4.3 introduces a control for family wealth, since party identification might also be associated with family wealth.

1. How does the original pattern seen in Table 4.2 change when we examine the two groups in Table 4.3?

2. Is the relationship between party identification and education affected by income?

3. What do the results in Table 4.3 indicate about the relationship between education and party identification?

4. Can you think of any logical explanation for the patterns displayed in the tables? What variable(s) is/are dependent? What variable(s) is/are independent? Why?

OUTLINE

CHAPTER FIVE

MEASURING VARIABLES AND RELATIONSHIPS

"He that makes Coates for the Moone, had need take measure every noone."

NATHANIEL WARD

Scientists basically measure three things: *variables, the chances that data about variables are meaningful,* and *relationships between variables.* Each of these measurement tasks has distinctive approaches and statistical devices. As we look at the ideas used in accomplishing these tasks, remember that measurement almost always looks more precise than it really is.

The term "measurement" will be used rather broadly in this chapter. For the first topic, the measurement of variance, we will examine the kinds of measurement suited to different types of variables. Next, we will look at techniques for describing the significance and representativeness of data obtained through scientific procedures. There are techniques for making fairly precise judgments about the chances that a set of data may be simply the result of a freakish sample rather than a meaningful measurement. In this connection, we show how sample surveys are constructed and discuss some common polling errors. Then, we present some ideas about measuring relationships *between* variables. The objective is to grasp the basic tools for reducing data about two or more related variables into a statistic that characterizes the relationship between them.

Conventionally, measurement as a term applies only to the first of these topics. The second concerns the problem of the significance and representativeness of data and uses probability, which isn't, in the narrowest sense, a form of measurement. The third is often seen as a question of characterizing the association between things rather than of measurement strictly speaking. Yet all three topics have to do with establishing quantities of something: variance, significance, and association. Consequently, all three topics have been fitted under the general rubric of measurement.

Measuring Variables: Levels of Measurement

Measurement is a deceptive subject. At first, it seems simple—measurement answers the question, "How much?" This appears easy enough to answer when talking about length or weight, but not so easy when considering such common fodder for social science as information levels, personal characteristics, feelings, and attitudes. The reason for the difficulty resides not so much in the matter of counting up units of things as in the nature of the things being counted.

In measuring variables, for example, two considerations determine what level of measurement can be attempted and, therefore, what sort of hypothetical relationships can be formulated using the variable. The considerations are:

1. The *properties* or characteristics of the variable
2. The measurement *technique* appropriate to these properties
3. The *levels* of measurement that are possible in view of the variable's properties and available techniques

Consider, for example, a variable such as *marital status*. The variable refers to a classification according to a legal definition: single (with the subdivisions of unmarried, divorced, widowed) or married (with perhaps the subdivision of monogamous or polygamous). In "measuring" someone's marital status, the property of the variable dictates that you can't do more than categorize—it's not possible to say that someone is very much married or very little married. In the eyes of the law, you either are or are not married. Given such a *property*, the variable *marital status* doesn't call for very fancy measurement *technique*.

The variable *intelligence* poses different possibilities for measurement. The *properties* of the variable do not limit consideration to mere classification: the variable has properties that imply larger and smaller amounts. This is where *technique* comes in. People have puzzled for centuries over how to measure intelligence. Efforts have included tests such as the sense to come in out of the rain—in which case intelligence can be measured in two categories: those who do, and those who don't, have the sense to come in out of the rain. Research marches on, however, and we have the IQ test. The IQ test gives us a reading on how well people can answer certain kinds of questions that are thought to have something to do with intelligence. This advance in technique permits fairly detailed gradations between the low and high ends of a scale associated with intelligence.

Measurement comprises an area of research all by itself. Researchers keep trying to develop measurement techniques that can explore all the properties of important variables. In order to systematize our understanding of various kinds of possible measurements, scientists have come up with a classification of the levels of measurement. The four levels are:

Nominal
Ordinal
Interval
Ratio

In Figure 5.1 the characteristics of these levels are explored. The *nominal* level doesn't quite seem like measurement; it refers to classifications of things. Take ethnicity for an example. If Sinnikka is a Finn and Igor is a Russian, we have said something about the properties of each person in relation to a variable called *ethnicity.* That's measurement, but not very fancy measurement. We can't rate Finns above Russians (except according to some other variable, such as fondness for pickled herring—and even then, it would be close). Therefore classification, or nominal measurement, is all that the properties of *ethnicity* as a variable allow.[1] Nominal measurement, low grade as it is, pops up frequently in social science as the examples listed in the figure indicate: race, region, sex, occupation, and so on.

If the properties of the variable allow ordering as well as classification, the *ordinal* level of measurement can be attempted, provided the techniques are available. At this level, we can think in terms of a continuum—that is, an array that indicates variation, as opposed to simple classification. Class is one illustration, and socioeconomic standing is another. We can say that Alphonse is upper class, while Mack is lower class. These are classifications, but they are arranged in such a way as

[1]We could, *within* each ethnic group, identify on the basis of parentage what proportion of a person's heritage belongs to an ethnic grouping, but the notion of ethnicity itself is classificatory.

FIGURE 5.1 LEVELS OF MEASUREMENT

Level	Variable Properties Allow You To:	Illustration	Examples

1. Nominal — Classify

Illustration: ?

Examples: Ethnicity, race, region, sex, marital status, occupation, group affiliation

2. Ordinal — Classify, Order

Illustration (Russian / Finnish / Norwegian):
Igor — Lower Class
Sinnikka — Lower Middle Class / Middle Class
Olaf — Upper Middle Class / Upper Class
?

Examples: Class, socioeconomic standing, formal education

3. Interval — Classify, Order, Set standard units of distance

Illustration: 1000 B.C., 500 B.C., 0 ZERO (Arbitrary), 500 A.D., 1000 A.D., 1500 A.D., 2000 A.D., 2500 A.D., 3000 A.D.
?

Examples: Biblical time, Fahrenheit temperature

4. Ratio — Classify, Order, Set standard units of distance, Locate absolute zero

Illustration: 0 ZERO (True), $2,000, $4,000, $6,000, $8,000, $10,000, $12,000, $14,000, $16,000
?

Examples: Income, age, weight, distance

to link them on a continuum from lower to higher. Similarly with formal education: Angelina has a Ph.D., Mary a high school education, and Jane a grade school certificate. However, a Ph.D. isn't the same "distance" from a college degree as a high school diploma is from a grade school certificate. Ordering, yes; standard distance, no. The specification of distance— or, more generally, the amount of variation between cases—is an important step up in the realm of measurement. Distance affords a decided increase in the sophistication with which a variable can be measured and related to other variables.

If standard distance can be achieved, the next level of measurement enters the picture: *interval* measurement. Here, units can be identified that indicate how far each case is from each other case. That's reasonable, but there remains one of those technicalities that causes confusion of the mind. It has to do with absolute zero on a scale of measurement.

Interval measures do not have a true zero. What is a true zero? And what good is it? In the example of biblical time, the year "zero" doesn't mean that nothing happened before then. We don't really know where true zero is in history. Zero was established in relationship to the life of Christ for religious reasons and serves as a convenient reference point for counting forward and backward. The same is true of Fahrenheit temperature. You know that 0 degrees Fahrenheit doesn't represent a true zero because −23 degrees is a lot colder than 0 degrees.

A *ratio scale* does have a true zero. A ratio scale like distance is different from an interval scale because, for example, in a ratio scale zero inches means just that—no distance at all. There can't be less than zero distance, or less than zero weight, or less than zero bananas. That tells you the formal difference between a *true* zero and an *arbitrary* zero, or one that is made up for the sake of convenience.

But what good is a true zero? The answer has to do with what can be said in comparing observations on a ratio or an interval scale. If Hardy weighs 200 pounds and Laurel weighs

100 pounds (ratio scale), we can see that Hardy is twice as heavy as Laurel. But if the temperature is 50 degrees on Monday and 25 degrees on Wednesday (interval scale), can we really say that it was twice as hot on Monday as on Wednesday? You can try and get away with it, but you really shouldn't, because a comparision of that kind requires a *true* zero. You need to know what the total absence of heat is when making out that one day was twice as hot as another. Without a beginning point, *distances* can be established, but not *ratios.*

The reason for knowing these distinctions has to do with the kind of relationships that can be established statistically within and between variables. The job is to avoid comparision of apples and oranges. Statistics enter this text only in the form of ideas behind numbers—the arithmetic and the finer points of various statistical operations are left to more technical writings. Here we will content ourselves with a simple point (simple as statistics go). Roughly speaking:

Nominal measurement allows statistics having to do with frequency of cases in each classification (e.g., ethnicity: 10 Finns, 3 Russians).

Ordinal measurement allows statistics that describe the way the cases are ordered with respect to a variable (e.g., education: grade school, high school, college).

Interval measurement permits comparisions of quantitative differences among cases on a scale (e.g., time: 1950, 1990).

Ratio measurement permits comparisons of absolute distances between cases (e.g., money: $10, $20).[2]

---

[2]From Sidney Siegel, *Nonparametric Statistics for the Social Sciences* (New York: McGraw-Hill, 1956), p. 30. See also David Leege and Wayne Francis, *Political Research* (New York: Basic Books, 1974), pp. 287–316.

For those who are familiar with statistics, the following is a list of examples of statistics appropriate to each level:

Nominal: mode, frequency, contingency coefficient (*footnote continues*)

Because these levels of measurement are the key to how relations between variables can be approached, it is essential to figure out the appropriate level of measurement for each variable before proceeding with research. We will see the significance of levels of management spelled out in more detail as we turn to the problem of measuring variable *relationships* in the form of correlations.

Measuring the Significance and Representativeness of Data: Probability, Sampling, and Problems in Polling

We now turn to these topics that fit together not so much because of their general connection with measurement, but because they all relate to understanding the strengths and weaknesses of data that are to be analyzed. The topics are probability, sampling, and problems in polling.

To get hold of the statistical tools basic to scientific research, we need to become familiar with a new concept: *probability*. Probability occupies a far more important place in social science than the amount of space devoted to it in this book would suggest. Probability constitutes nothing less than a fundamental of the scientific perspective. To understand why is to come to grips with some particularly ornery habits of the human mind.

Probability refers to the likelihood or chance of something occurring. We compute probabilities about the chances of pass-

Ordinal: median, percentile, Spearman's *rho*, Kendall W, Goodman-Kruskal's *gamma*
Interval: mean, standard deviation, Pearson's product-moment correlation, multiple product-moment correlation
Ratio: geometric mean, coefficient of variation

ing a course, the prospects for a date, the odds of a team winning a game. That *Roget's Thesaurus* lists so many alternatives for the word "probability"—luck, hazard, fortuity, fate, contingency, chance, and others—indicates the importance of the concept in our language.

We began by saying that science becomes useful to human beings as a way of coping with the uncertainties of life. By forcing ideas and notions out of the head and into the arena of empirical observation and by testing them, we gain knowledge about the world. The scientific establishment is built on the power provided by the effort to escape the insecurity of uncertainty about our surroundings. However, it is characteristic of scientific knowledge that it is rarely cast in stone. Often explicitly and always implicitly, scientific generalizations are probabilistic.

Science is the refinement of chance far more often than the discovery of certainty. Indeed, social scientists often discuss their findings in a language that expresses the possibility of being wrong. We worry about the odds that a set of results reflects an inaccurate sample, or that another researcher would find different results from ours. Formally, we rarely speak of social science as conclusively *proving* anything.[3] Rather, we speak of the *probability* that a hypothesis is supported by the available evidence.

As an illustration of the way probability is built into social science, we shall consider two special applications of probability statistics: determining the statistical significance of an array of data, and constructing representative samples of larger

[3]An influential critique of positivism from within the philosophy of science can be found in W. V. O. Quine, "The Two Dogmas of Empiricism," *From a Logical Point of View*, ed. W. V. O. Quine (New York: Harper and Row, 1961). See also Alexander Rosenberg, *The Structure of Biological Science* (Cambridge: Cambridge University Press, 1985).

99

populations. Yet the objective is the same in both: trying to specify the odds that a display of data reveals something more than a chance relationship between variables. If the information is based on a faulty sample or if it represents merely a freak combination of cases, then the results can't be said to tell us anything conclusive about the relationship between the variables. It is important to know that, and probability statistics provide some tools.

The first usage of probability concerns the representativeness of a sample drawn from a larger population. Given the size and characteristics of a sample, what is the probability that we can *infer* from a sample some specific characteristic of a population? This form of probability underlies public opinion polling. Pollsters often try to estimate the percentage of the public that intends to vote for a specific candidate. In attempting to characterize the behavior of a huge group of people, it is nearly always impossible to survey everyone. Selecting the smallest, most representative possible sample is the key to efficiency in polling. Probability statistics are used to estimate the chances that a sample is representative.

The second application of probability involved estimating the likelihood of a set of observations occurring by chance. If there is only one chance in a hundred that the results we are seeing would have occurred randomly, then the pattern is quite significant. A pattern of data linking two variables (say, income and education) that has a chance of occurring randomly one time in a hundred tells us something useful. Without probing the mathematics, we would refer to this result as *significant at the .01 level*. Significance statistics are derived by combining the number of observations in the sample, the amount of variation in the variables, and the magnitude of the observed relationship. The most likely random distribution of results would show the same number of cases in each cell of a table; the least likely would have all the cases in one cell.

Establishing the level of significance of the results constitutes an important test of the hypothesis. Results demonstrating that all upper income people are highly educated, and that all lower income people are poorly educated, are most unlikely to occur by chance. The independent variable has a very strong impact on the dependent variable. There is very likely a correlation between income and education in the population. Significance tests tell us, under certain conditions, the probability that our hypothesis is right (or wrong).

In its most basic form, significance tells us "whether or not a certain relationship . . . is worth further thought—whether it might repay additional research effort."[4] Some social scientists will deal only with data significant at the .01 level, whereas others accept .05 as the cutoff—meaning that there are five chances (as opposed to one chance) out of 100 of the observed relationship occurring by chance. The significance level is commonly noted as part of a research report, which helps in evaluating results.

The two uses of probability we have been discussing are related: the first deals with whether the sample is representative, and the second concerns the chances that the results are meaningful. Loosely stated, the questions become:

Is the sample representative? [inference]
Is the pattern of results likely to have occurred by chance? [significance]

A representative sample provides a sound basis for inferring the level of support for a hypothesis, especially if the

---

[4]For a lucid and accessible discussion of significance testing, see Lawrence Mohr, *Understanding Significance Tests*, Sage University Paper Series on Quantitative Applications in Social Science no. 73 (Beverly Hills, Calif.: 1990).

pattern of observations is statistically significant. A poor sample, however, will make for poor inferences whether or not the pattern of data is significant. A sample drawn according to probability theory is known, not surprisingly, as a *probability sample*.

There are two general techniques used in sampling: *stratification* and *randomization*. Stratification involves trying to reproduce a large population by representing important characteristics proportionately in the sample. If we tried to determine a community's attitude toward drinking by interviewing a sample of customers at a local saloon, that sample would overrepresent one segment of the public in terms of a characteristic vital to the issue under consideration. Teetotalers don't hang out in saloons. Therefore, we would have to select the sample in such a way that teetotalers have a chance of being included.

If the stratification method were used to select a sample for determining voting behavior in an election, we would try to have a sample that reflected proportionately the larger population at least in terms of such significant independent variables as class, region, and education. However, the stratification (proportionate sampling of certain characteristics of voters) must be limited to a relatively small number of characteristics. Otherwise, in order to fill out the sample with representatives of all the variables in the proper proportion, we might wind up spending valuable resources trying to find people with highly unlikely combinations of characteristics.

Random sampling depends on selecting at random a sufficient sample of the population such that there is a high probability of reproducing the essential characteristics of the total population. The likelihood of representativeness increases in predictable fashion as the size of the sample grows. For example, if we interview five randomly selected people out of a national population of 210 million, the chances are not so good that they are truly representative—there would be a very high margin of error. With each increase in the size of the sample, provided the people are selected randomly, the margin of error decreases.

For any size population, it is possible to determine mathematically the probability that a given sample size will generate a specifiable margin of error. The margin of error drops drastically with the increasing size of the sample, up to a point at which further increases in sample size reduce the margin of error very little. It is this point that indicates the most economical sample size. By doubling or tripling the sample size beyond this point, or even multiplying it by 10, relatively little reduction of error can be achieved.

One major problem with random sampling is that in order to interview all of those who are selected, the interviewers have to disperse their efforts and seek out respondents in all corners of the total population. Most scientific sampling uses both stratification and randomization. For example, in a national sample, one might select representative urban areas and representative rural areas (a form of stratification) and then draw a random sample within those target areas.

Telephone sampling, though it contains a bias against those who have no phones, has become an increasingly popular technique now that computers make it possible to do random digit dialing withing specific telephone exchanges. Evolutions in communications technology are introducing new biases to phone sampling, however. Pagers, beepers, and answering machines are hooked up on many telephone exchanges. Annoyance with heavy telemarketing efforts might be boosting refusal rates for survey researchers. Good phone samples may still be drawn, but costs are increasing as researchers act to minimize these new biases.

For their surveys of American opinion, Gallup and Harris and the major media polls (CBS/*New York Times*, ABC/*Washington Post*, *USA Today*/CNN) use a stratified random sample so as to eliminate, among other problems, the inconvenience of interviewing a randomly selected sheepherder in a remote section of Nevada. The sample size is typically about 1500 persons. At this size, the margin of error is about 3 percent at the .05 level of significance. What this means is that for 95 samples out of 100, the opinions expressed by those in the sample will reflect the whole population within a range of plus or minus 3 percent. So if a given sample illustrates that 49 percent of the people plan to vote Republican for president, 95 samples out of 100 would show the Republican candidate getting somewhere between 46 percent and 52 percent of the vote if the election were held on the day of the poll.

Both Gallup and Harris have a very impressive record of achievement in using samples of this kind to predict presidential elections, in part because they have been lucky in not drawing a "way-out" sample, one of the five in a hundred, and in part because they do stratify their samples somewhat to avoid the weird sample that might occur if simple random sampling were used.

Another way of understanding sampling is to consider how poor samples lead to faulty conclusions. Bad samples have led to some major mistakes in forecasting presidential elections. A now-defunct publication, the *Literary Digest*, made itself famous by surveying millions of voters per election and forecasting (accurately) the presidential elections of 1924, 1928, and 1932. The accuracy of these forecasts was attributed by many people to the sheer size of the sample. However, the *Digest* mailed surveys to people drawn from lists of car and telephone owners—a method that ran a serious risk in the 1920s and 1930s of underrepresenting the less affluent. After surveying over two million voters in 1936, the *Literary Digest* inferred from its sample that Alf Landon would defeat President Roosevelt, with Landon getting 57 percent of the vote. President Landon? It didn't happen. Landon received only 36 percent of the vote in the election.

TABLE 5.1   TAXING AND SPENDING: THE EFFECTS OF
SAMPLE BIAS

Question 1: Do you believe that for every dollar of tax increase there should be $2 in spending cuts with the savings earmarked for deficit and debt reduction?

	Yes	No	No Answer
TV Guide Mail-In Response	97%	na	na
Yankelovich National Sample	67	18	15

Question 2: Should laws be passed to eliminate all possibilities of special interests giving huge sums of money to candidates?

	Yes	No	No Answer
TV Guide Mail-In Response	99%	na	na
Yankelovich National Sample	80	17	3

SOURCE: *The Public Perspective*, May/June 1993, as reported in the *New York Times*, September 7, 1993, p. B8.

It should be stressed that a large sample will not necessarily compensate for unrepresentativeness.[5]

Techniques such as stratified random sampling have greatly improved the reliability of polls; however, candidates and interest groups sometimes conduct surveys that replicate the mistakes of the *Digest* polls. Consider the data shown in Table 5.1. During the 1992 presidential campaign, Ross Perot's organization mailed out surveys in *TV Guide* magazine and asked readers to mark their ballots as they watched a televised address by the candidate. Responses were then mailed back to Perot's organization. Yet when another group drew random probability samples and respondents were given the same questions, results differed

---

[5]The 1936 election made George Gallup famous. He used a much smaller and relatively random "quota" sample to predict that Roosevelt would win. For an account of polling in this election, see David W. Moore, *The Superpollsters* (New York: Four Walls Eight Windows, 1992). Gallup's 1936 "quota" method caused another famous failure, however, when his sample led him to predict that Dewey would defeat Truman in 1948. Since 1948, Gallup and other pollsters have come to use probability samples.

TABLE 5.2   COMMON SOURCES OF ERROR

Error	*Example*
Ambiguous questions:	Do you think we ought to strive for peace or for a strong defense?
Symbolically loaded questions that elicit biased answers:	Do you think unborn children have a right to life? / Do you think pregnant women should have the right to choose an abortion? versus Do you favor or oppose legal abortion?
Difficult questions beyond the information level of the respondent:	Do you approve or disapprove of the ballistic missile sections of the position taken by the United States in the disarmament negotiations with Russia?
Response alternatives unsuited to the subject of the question:	Do you feel better or worse about the future?
Questions that include more than one issue:	Are you more likely to favor a candidate who supports busing and a strong defense or one who has a pleasing personality?

substantially from those reported by the Perot organization.[6] The Perot data suffered from the error of *sample bias;* no real attempts at randomization or stratification were made. Consequently, this poll could not be presented as a credible representation of public opinion.

It should be noted that there are other sources of error that creep into survey research besides the representativeness of the sample. A researcher may have selected a highly representative sample, but his or her instruments of measurement may elicit misleading answers. Common sources of error include those presented in Table 5.2.

[6]Daniel Goleman, "Pollsters Enlist Psychologists in Quest for Unbiased Results," *New York Times*, September 7, 1993, pp. B5, B8. Also see *The Public Perspective* (Roper Center for Public Opinion Research), May/June 1993.

"Mr. Perot states, 'It's time to take out the trash
and clean out the barn.' Agree or disagree?"

Drawing by D. Reilly; © 1992 The New Yorker Magazine, Inc.

Beyond these obvious kinds of error, there is a whole category of errors that enters into research design; these errors
arise from the difficulty of being sure you are measuring what
you think you are measuring. An example would be a question
developed out of an interest in understanding people's personal
sympathies for the poor: Do you approve or disapprove of poor
persons stealing bread when they are hungry? Someone who
has enormous sympathy for the poor might say "I disapprove,"
because that person, while sympathizing with the poor very
strongly, also has enormous respect for law and order. Note that

the question is not meaningless; the error comes from attributing an inappropriate meaning to the responses. The question taps another variable, *respect for law and order,* in addition to the one intended, *attitudes toward the poor.*

Added to errors arising from sloppy measurement are errors introduced by the statistical procedures used to characterize the data. Statistics always distort reality to at least a small degree—that is why statisticians prefer using several techniques for characterizing data so as to hedge against the bias of a single procedure.

Measuring Relationships between Variables: Association and Correlation

Association

Establishing the degree of association between two or more variables gets at the central objective of the scientific enterprise. Scientists spend most of their time figuring out how one thing relates to another and structuring these relationships into explanatory theories.

As with other forms of measurement, the question of association comes up frequently in normal discourse, as in: "like father, like son"; "if you've seen one, you've seen 'em all"; "an orange a day keeps the scurvy away." In measuring the degree of association between variables statistically, scientists are merely doing what science is famous for: being rigorous and precise about a commonplace activity.

Association can sometimes be characterized in simple ways. The effects of one variable on another can be described in words or by statistics. "People who use Crest have fewer cavities" is a statement that presents a relationship between an independent variable, *brushing with Crest,* and a dependent variable, *number of cavities.*

Descriptive statistics like the median, the average, and the standard deviation can be employed effectively in specifying association. For example, in the study entitled "Schematic Assessments of Presidential Candidates" (see Appendix A), the number of comments about "competence" was averaged for each education level. This permits analysis of the influence of education on candidate assessments.[7] Percentage differences are also handy comparative instruments. For example, if 99 percent of those on the crew of the *Santa Maria* who ate an orange every day didn't get scurvy, and if 60 percent of those who ate no oranges (or any other fruit) *did* get scurvy, we can say that the chances of getting scurvy were vastly reduced by regular orange eating.

Measures of Association and Correlation

For certain applications, statisticians have developed more sophisticated tools for specifying relationships between variables: measures of association and correlation. Variables measured at different levels require that different statistics be used to test for association. The result is a Greek alphabet-soup of tests that tend to share a common logic.

Measures of association and correlation are usually approached as a statistical matter; here we will concentrate on the ideas behind them. Our discussion should help you recognize a correlation statistic when you see one. To understand the arithmetic and the limiting assumptions, you may consult a statistics text.

The essential idea of correlation is to describe statistically the association between variables. Assuming all other conditions are equal, measures of association summarize the movement of two variables in relation to each other.

---

[7]See Appendix A, "Schematic Assessments of Presidential Candidates."

Correlation analysis is an advance over comparing percentage differences because it allows you to capture in a single statistic both the *direction* and the *amount* of association. *Direction* refers to whether the association is *positive* or *negative*. A positive correlation exists when, as variable A increases, variable B also increases. That is, variable A goes up as variable B goes up (or vice versa). A negative correlation exists when, as variable A changes, variable B changes in the opposite direction. In the case of a negative correlation, as A increases, B decreases (or, as A decreases, B increases).

For example, there is a positive correlation between the quantity of helium in a balloon and the rate at which the balloon rises. There is a negative correlation between the rate of rise and the weight of the balloon. The positive/negative direction is expressed by a + or − before the correlation figure.

The strength of a correlation is expressed by the size of the number on a scale from zero to +1.00 or −1.00. The scale is illustrated in Figure 5.2. Thus, correlation statistics provide simple indexes of relationships between variables and measures of association—a dangerously simple scheme, for the mathematics behind these statistics involves assumptions that require careful thought. In addition, the variety of techniques by which measures of association are computed causes the results to deviate slightly from the reality of the data. Understanding the general techniques by which correlation operates will allow you to see some, though not all, of the problems. Nevertheless, in the imperfect world of measurement, these statistics are valuable tools.

The techniques for computing measures of association vary with the level of measurement used. If two variables are measured on a nominal scale (classification only), there is less that can be done to characterize association than would be the case with two variables measured on an interval scale. In fact, there

110

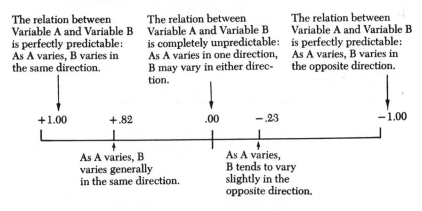

FIGURE 5.2   THE SCALE OF CORRELATION

The relation between Variable A and Variable B is perfectly predictable: As A varies, B varies in the same direction.

The relation between Variable A and Variable B is completely unpredictable: As A varies in one direction, B may vary in either direction.

The relation between Variable A and Variable B is perfectly predictable: As A varies, B varies in the opposite direction.

+1.00   +.82   .00   −.23   −1.00

As A varies, B varies generally in the same direction.

As A varies, B tends to vary slightly in the opposite direction.

are correlation techniques available for every level of measurement, and we will describe generally how they work.

Nominal-Level Association   Nominal measurement, involving only simple classification, is low-grade stuff and the measure of association appropriate to it really doesn't deserve to be called correlation. The *contingency coefficient* is a statistic often used to summarize how far the actual distribution of data deviates from a distribution in which one variable is associated with no change in the other.

Suppose a researcher wishes to test the proposition stated in the title of a Steve Martin movie, *Dead Men Don't Wear Plaid.* In order to be thorough, the researcher decides to check on the relative incidence of plaid-wearing among dead as well as living men, to see if being deceased really does make a difference—speaking sartorially. The researcher views a random sample of twenty living men and checks the local funeral parlor for twenty deceased males. If it turns out that men wear plaid just as often alive as dead, then Martin's hypothesis isn't worth much.

Table 5.3 presents a set of results showing no association

TABLE 5.3   EXPECTED INCIDENCE OF
PLAID-WEARING

Pattern of Clothing	Condition of Men	
	Living	Dead
Plaid	12	12
Non-Plaid	8	8

TABLE 5.4   OBSERVED INCIDENCE OF
PLAID-WEARING

Pattern of Clothing	Condition of Men	
	Living	Dead
Plaid	5	14
Non-plaid	15	6

between wearing plaid and being dead or alive. This is what we might see if there were no association between the two variables. The figures show that 24 plaid-wearing men are evenly divided among the living and the dead. Similarly, 16 non-plaid wearing men are also as likely living as dead. In this case the contingency coefficient would be zero.

But suppose we actually observe something else. What if there were differences in the amount of plaid-wearing among dead men as opposed to living men? How could this be expressed in precise statistical terms?

The contingency coefficient is computed by comparing a distribution of (1) what we would *expect* to see in a table if there were no association (Table 5.3), to (2) what we actually might *observe* (Table 5.4). The results in Table 5.3 can be expressed as either a chi-square [pronounced *kye-square*] statistic or a contingency coefficient. Since chi-square has no upper limit, for the sake of interpretation it is often converted into statistics such as the contingency coefficient (which ranges from zero to slightly less than zero, with larger values reflecting greater association). If, in fact, the distribution was found as shown in Table 5.3,[8] then chi-square would equal 8.12, and the contingency coefficient would be .41. These statistics point to an association between corporeal condition and clothing—but it isn't the one suggested in the movie title. It appears that a greater proportion of dead men wear plaid than living men.

In more systematic language, this sort of distribution indicates some association between being deceased and wearing a certain pattern of clothing—in this case, plaid. The contingency coefficient is used to characterize the association between two non-orderable, nominal-level variables.[9] This measure ranges from -1.0 to $+1.0$. Remember, a minus statistic indicates that as one variable increases, the other decreases (or vice versa). A plus statistic means that the variation is in the same direction for both variables. When the possibility exists of ordering as well as classifying the categories in the variable, establishing genuine correlation becomes possible.

Ordinal-Level Correlation Ordinal stands for order. It is this characteristic that supplies the basis for Spearman's rank correlation coefficient (*rho*) and other statistics that can be computed at the ordinal level. What can be done is to compare the ranking of cases according to their ordering on two variables. An illustration will help.

Imagine a group of 160 Jaycees singing "God Bless America." The song leader, a systematic person who is secretly a Marxist, rates the singers according to four categories of musical ability from best to worst: Canaries, Robins, Sparrows, and Crows. He wishes to test his belief that lower-class folks are better singers than the upper crust.

---

[8]See G. W. Bohrnstedt and D. Knoke, *Statistics for Social Data Analysis* (Itasca, Ill.: F. E. Peacock, 1988), p. 310.

[9]Other chi-square based statistics that assess association among variables measured at this level on a scale of zero to one are Cramer's *v* and *phi*.

So he has two ordered classifications to work with: *musical ability* ordered in terms of Canaries, Robins, Sparrows, and Crows; and *class* ordered in terms of upper, upper middle, lower middle, and lower. The hypothesis he wishes to test is whether there is any association between socioeconomic class and musical ability. The songmaster hypothesizes that lower-class people sing better than upper-class people.

If that were true, the data would show a certain pattern. As class went up, musical ability would go down. The lower classes would be heavily populated with Canaries, and the upper classes with Crows. Suppose he found the distribution presented in Table 5.5.

The relationship is not crystal clear from the data, but we can see that there is a pronounced tendency for lower-class Jaycees to warble more sweetly than their "betters." Now we need a statistic that helps nail down the degree of association. Goodman-Kruskal's *gamma,* among other similar statistics, uses an interesting logic to summarize the degree of association. *Gamma* reflects the proportion of reduction in errors in predicting rankings on our dependent variable (musical ability), given knowledge of the ranked distribution of the independent variable (class). If the person's class predicted singing ability perfectly, *gamma* would be high; if not, *gamma* would be low.

Returning to the hypothesis: As we go up the class scale,

TABLE 5.5 MUSICAL ABILITY BY CLASS

Ability	Upper Class	Upper Middle Class	Lower Middle Class	Lower Class
Canaries	0	0	5	30
Robins	0	10	20	10
Sparrows	5	15	15	0
Crows	35	15	0	0

do the data indicate that there is a corresponding fall-off in the musical-ability scale? In the data presented in Table 5.5, the *gamma* would be −.93. This means that if we know a person's class, it improves our ability of predicting a person's ranking on musical ability by 93 percent (as compared with predicting musical ability knowing nothing about a person's class). Does this affirm the hypothesis? Yes. There is a negative association between class level and ability to sing.

Interval- and Ratio-Level Correlation To do interval or ratio measurement, you need to be able to establish distances between the units of analysis. It isn't good enough to have singers arrayed in terms of Canaries, Robins, Sparrows, and Crows; the amount of distance between Canaries and Robins and the rest has to be specified. The difference in singing ability between Canaries and Robins may be quite unlike the difference between Sparrows and Crows. With the specification of distance comes the possibility of using a correlation statistic that employs the factor of distance to measure the association between variables.

Interval and ratio measurements allow the use of a formidable-sounding statistic by the name of Pearson's product-moment correlation coefficient (Pearson's *r*).

To keep things simple, we will make up a very elementary example: the relationship in the sheikdom of Exxit between the number of oil wells owned and the number of Cadillacs. Our "sample" consists of five oil-well owners. To see what the mathematics of the Pearson's product-moment correlation accomplishes, consider two possible arrays of data. Suppose, first of all, that there is a correlation of +1.00 between number of oil wells and number of Cadillacs. Figure 5.3 illustrates two sets of data for which that same correlation of +1.00 could be claimed.

Notice the straight solid line that can be drawn connecting each case expressing the following relationship between the two variables: as oil wells increase by one, Cadillacs increase by

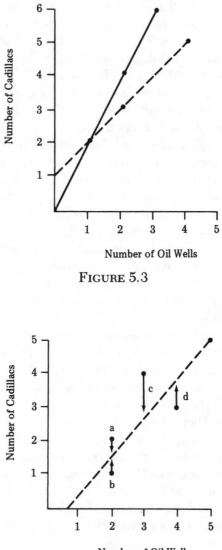

FIGURE 5.3

FIGURE 5.4

two. A perfect correlation also results if the straight line should happen to fall on a different level; for example, see the broken line. It shows that you can get a Cadillac without an oil well, but for every extra Cadillac, it appears necessary to sink a new well.

Now imagine an array of data in which the cases do *not* present themselves on a straight line. If the data were to appear as in Table 5.6 and Figure 5.4, no straight line can be drawn that connects all the cases. Pearson's *r* by a mathematical process identifies the line that most closely expresses the linear relationship. It is the one straight line that is closest to all the points on the chart—the line that minimizes the distance by which all the cases deviate from the line. For mathematical reasons (best left to mathematicians), the deviations of cases from the line are measured in terms of the squares of the distances $(a^2 + b^2 + c^2 + d^2)$ rather than simple distances $(a + b + c + d)$. The more distant the cases are from the best-fitting line, the lower the correlation of variable A with variable B. The Pearson's *r* for Figure 5.4 is +.85.

The Pearson correlation statistic can be made to supply one other important piece of information. By squaring Pearson's *r*, we can find out what proportion of all the variation in the dependent variable is explained by variation in the independent variable. In the case of oil wells and Cadillacs in Figure 5.4, Pearson's *r* is +.85, so r^2 is .72 (.85 × .85). Thus, the number of oil wells a person has explains 72 percent of the variation in the number of Cadillacs owned. Other variables explain the remaining 28 percent of the variation.

Alternatively, if all of the points fell on the line (as in Figure 5.3) and *r* is +1.00, then r^2 would also be 1.00 (i.e. 1 × 1 = 1)! The number of oil wells correlates perfectly with the number of Cadillacs, and there is no variation left over to be explained by other factors.

As with each of the measures of association discussed here, Pearson's *r* tells us about correlation, which may

117

or may not indicate a causal relationship. A significant *r* does *not* show that the number of oil wells *causes* people to own more Cadillacs, only that the two things go together. The actual relationship might be reversed (although, in this example, that might seem illogical). We might find that two things are correlated yet have no clear-cut idea about which variable determines the other. Suppose a researcher finds that educational attainment is correlated with intellgence. Which causes which? Measures of association do not require that the researcher assume anything about causation. Statistics do not establish causation; *causation depends on the logic of relationships* (see Table 4.4).

Notice what else this procedure does *not* accomplish. A Pearson's *r* of +1.00 indicates only that any variation in A is associated with a consistent variation in B. What it does *not* tell you is the number of units B varies in relation to A. It happens in the example in Figure 5.3 (solid line) that as oil wells go up by one, Cadillacs go up by two. But if the situation were such that for *every* increase of one oil well there was a consistent increase of one Cadillac, or ½ of a Cadillac, or three Cadillacs, a +1.00 result would be obtained.

In mathematical terms, Pearson's *r* tells you only about the dispersion of cases around an imaginary straight line. It does *not* tell you the slope of the line—or, in other words, the *amount* of change in B for every unit of variation in A. A sepa-

TABLE 5.6

Number of Cadillacs	*Number of Oil Wells*				
	One	*Two*	*Three*	*Four*	*Five*
One	1				
Two	1				
Three				1	
Four		1			
Five					1

rate statistical procedure involving advanced statistical concepts called *regression analysis* deals with this question.

Regression Analysis

The purpose of this general kind of measurement is to characterize the impact of variables on each other. Regression analysis adds a new level of sophistication to these characterizations. With regression, if you know the value of an independent variable, you can begin to predict the value of the dependent variable.

There are two basic forms of regression: *bivariate* regression and *multiple* regression. Bivariate regression, like correlation analysis, characterizes how changes in levels of a single independent variable are related to change in a dependent variable. Multiple regression examines how several different independent variables are associated with a dependent variable.

As an example of bivariate regression, consider a simple example from major league baseball. Since professional baseball teams spend differing amounts of money on player salaries, we might wonder whether higher levels of spending are associated with how teams finish in the division standings. How much of an effect does *spending* have on *finish?* Bivariate regression helps to answer this question by summarizing the association between the two variables in terms of the following linear equation:

$$Y \text{ [team finish]} = a + bX \text{ [spending]}$$

Expressing the association in words, values on the Y variable (*team finish*) are a function of some constant, plus some amount of the X variable. The question we are interested in is *how much* change in the Y variable (*finish*) is associated with a one unit change in the X variable (*spending*). That answer lies in *b*; this is

119

known as the *regression coefficient*.[10] In terms of the baseball example, it would be the amount of improvement in finish associated with an additional one million dollars in spending on players' salaries.

We can use data from the 1993 season to test the hypothesis that spending affects team finish.[11] We measure spending (the X variable) in millions of dollars, and team finish (the Y variable) as 1 = first, 2 = second . . . 7 = last. Pearson's *r* correlation between the two variables is −.60, suggesting that as a teams spend more money, they finish closer to first. A bivariate regression shows that

$$\text{team division finish} = 7.4 - 0.112 \times \text{spending}$$

This means that the slope of the relationship between spending and finish is negative 0.112. Or, for each million dollars that a team spends, there is about a tenth of a place (0.112) change in Y (division position). The results, moreover, are significant at the .001 level.

We can use these results to show that a team spending $50 million on players will very likely finish in at least second place (7.4 − 0.112 × $50m = 1.8). We can also show that a team would probably have to spend about $9 million more to move one position (−0.112 × $9m = 1.008).[12]

What about regression that involves more than one vari-

[10]In alegebraic terms, *b* represents the slope of the relationship between X and Y. Mixing algebra with baseball, *b* would be the "rise over the run" if we were to plot the relationship between Y and X on a graph.

[11]Data drawn from Murray Chass, "Yankees Attain Dubious Advantage over Jays," *New York Times*, November 12, 1993, p. B13.

[12]The constant, or intercept of the Y axis (7.4) represents what the value of Y would be if X were zero (in this case, last place!). Since Pearson's *r* for this example was −.60, we know that spending explains 36 percent of the variation in the team's finishes ($r^2 = .36 = -.60 \times -.60$).

able (and what about an example that relates directly to politics?). As an example of *multiple regression,* suppose you notice that your friends differ widely in their level of involvement in electoral politics. Activity might range across a spectrum as illustrated below:

nonvoters   occasional voters   party activists

Why are some people more active than others? Factors that occur prior to, or independently of, activism would include income levels, education levels, or levels of prior experience with politics (call them independent variables). Each could logically be associated with the level of activism. Multiple regression permits analysis of the effects of several independent variables at the same time. This technique isolates the effect of a single independent variable while controlling for (or holding constant) the effects of other independent variables.

To pursue the example, political activism, the dependent variable, could be operationalized in terms of a score derived from the number of political activities a person is involved in: voting, campaigning, contributing to candidates, engaging in protests or demonstrations, and so on. The more activities engaged in, the higher the participation score. Measurements for each of the independent variables could be similarly constructed.

As we have seen, measures of correlation make it possible to see whether income and political participation, for example, are positively or negatively related (whether participation goes up or down as income rises). Correlation also establishes how closely one varies in association with the other.

With a knowledge of the correlation of income and participation, you can estimate whether a rich person is more or less likely to be politically active than a poor person. If, however, you would like to have a better chance of predicting the amount of change in participation associated with each change in level of income, then regression analysis is required. To test for the effect of one independent variable on a dependent variable while controlling for the effects of one or more additional variables, multiple regression is required.

For example, we might expect that variation in activism is associated with both income and education. Multiple regression estimates statistically the unique effect of each variable on the dependent variable while holding other independent variables constant. Thus, we can see if education affects participation while controlling for income levels. Multiple regression tables typically report a series of b's (slopes, or regression coefficients) for each of the independent variables included in the analysis. These are interpreted as the amount of change in the dependent (Y) variable associated with a one unit change in an independent variable (X_1) while holding other included variables (X_2, X_3, etc.) constant.

Recall the brief discussion about control and spuriousness from Chapter 4. Social scientists are often unable to use laboratories to control or "hold constant" the effects of multiple variables. It would be impossible as well as cruel, for example, to randomly distribute certain levels of income to different people, randomly distribute certain levels of education to people, then place them in a laboratory and wait to observe if participation occurs at different rates among people with different mixes of income and education. For this reason, social scientists often measure existing phenomena and then use statistical procedures such as multiple regression to control for the effects of variables that cannot (or should not) be manipulated.[13]

---

[13]A treatment of the mathematics of regression is beyond the scope of this book. But there are countless texts available on the topic. Brief, accessible introductions can be found in L. Schroeder, D. Sjoquist, and P. Stephan, *Understanding Regression Analysis*, Sage University Paper Series on Quantitative Applications in Social Science no. 57 (Beverly Hills, Calif.: 1986); or M. Lewis-Beck, *Applied Regression*, Sage University Paper Series on Quantitative Applications in Social Science no. 22 (Beverly Hills, Calif: 1980).

Interpreting multiple regression coefficients can become complicated when the independent variables are measured in different units. Since measures of income (dollars) range much more widely than measures of education (years of schooling), it is hard to compare the two variables. But there is a statistical technique for making them comparable. The units can be expressed in terms of *standard deviation* units. A variable that has a lot of cases that are at the high and low ends of variation, regardless of how great the range of variation is, will have a large standard deviation. A variable for which the scores concentrate around the average will have a low standard deviation. This method of standardizing is used often in regression analysis.[14]

The resulting standardized regression coefficient is typically referred to as the *Beta coefficient;* and like the Pearson's *r*, it usually varies from −1.00 to +1.00. For example, if we found that the Beta coefficient for income was +1.00, this would indicate that a one standard deviation unit change in income is associated with a one standard deviation unit change in participation. If we found the Beta to be +.50, we would conclude that a one standard deviation unit change in income is associated with one-half a standard deviation change in participation.

The regression coefficient and Betas are one part of regression analysis. The other part is a multiple correlation statistic, *R* (not to be confused with Pearson's small *r*, which deals with a single independent variable). *R* reports the correlation between a group of independent variables and a dependent variable. And, in parallel fashion there is R^2, which indicates the proportion of the variation in the dependent variable explained

---

[14]There are a number of technical problems associated with using standardized regression coefficients. Some scholars suggest that findings should simply be expressed in terms of "real" units. See Gary King, "How Not to Lie with Statistics," *American Journal of Political Science* 30 (1986): 666–687.

by the group of independent variables under consideration. Table 5.7 should help unscramble these statistics.

Taking the two measures together as multiple regression analysis, we can say that if Beta $= +.5$, every increase of one unit of income associates with a half-unit increase in political activism. However, if $R = .56$, only about half of the variation in activism is explained by income. Were we to project from income to activism, we would know roughly where a given income level would place someone on an activism scale, while recognizing that other variables would be required to predict the participation level more precisely.

As a way of summarizing what has been presented so far

TABLE 5.7   MEASURES OF ASSOCIATION, CORRELATION, AND REGRESSION

Statistic[a]	*Meaning*
r	*Pearson's correlation coefficient:* the degree of covariance between two variables (-1.00 to $+1.00$)
r^2	*Coefficient of determination:* in bivariate regression, the proportion of the variation in a dependent variable explained by the changes in the independent variable (0 to $+1.00$)
R	*Multiple correlation statistic:* the degree of covariance in a dependent variable associated with changes in two or more independent variables (0 to $+1.00$)
R^2	*Coefficient of determination:* the proportion of the variation in a dependent variable explained by changes in two or more independent variables (1 to $+1.00$)
b	*Unstandardized regression coefficient:* the amount of variation in a dependent variable that occurs with each unit of variation in the independent variable (zero to infinity)
Beta	*Standardized regression coefficient:* the amount of variation in a dependent variable for each unit of variation in one or more independent variables where the units of all variables are made comparable in terms of standard deviations from the mean (usually varies between -1.00 and $+1.00$)

[a]For purposes of this table, we are using Pearson's r as the only measure of correlation. For other measures, see footnote 2.

about measuring relationships between variables and to set the agenda for the remaining discussion, look at Table 5.7.

Why Multiple Regression? Control and Spuriousness

How do you establish the unique effect of one independent variable while the effects of others are held constant? Multiple regression analysis is the answer.

Recall that in Chapter 3 (and in Appendix A), Arthur Miller et al. were interested in whether better educated people assess candidates differently than those who have less education. They suggest that education is associated with the ability to evaluate candidates in terms of complex abstractions like integrity and competence rather than personal appearance. A quick look at the results in Table 3.2 suggests that people with a college education are more likely to comment on these dimensions. Does this mean that education *causes* people to think about candidates in abstract terms? The answer appears to be yes, but there could be a problem. A third variable might affect the relationship between *education* and *assessments of candidates*. It might be that the pattern we see in Table 3.2 is produced by the influence of a third variable that is not accounted for. This is the problem of *spuriousness*.

A result is said to be spurious if it can be explained away by another variable. A classic example of a spurious relationship is the high correlation between the *number of fire trucks* at the scene of a fire and the *amount of damage* caused by the fire. The conclusion seems simple: additional trucks cause more damage! The omitted variable, of course, is the *size of the fire*. A bigger fire brings out more trucks *and* causes more damage.

To return to the question of candidate assessments, what if educated people simply talk more than less educated people? In answering the open-ended questions asked by Miller and his associates, maybe educated people were more talkative rather than more sophisticated. This verbosity might well be associated with a college education. Perhaps educated respondents offer more assessments, but they may not necessarily use complex reasoning. One fundamental goal of any scientific endeavor is to *control* for other variables that might explain away an important result.

In this example, Miller et al. use multiple regression to statistically control for the fact that some people talk more than others. It turns out that the relationship between education and assessments remains significant even when they control for the effect of the variable *articulateness*. In your own research you might not use advanced statistics or laboratory experiments to control for any omitted variables that could explain away your observations. Nevertheless, you should consider discussing how confident you are that your results are not spurious.

To take the discussion a few steps further, let's look at another example. In Appendix B, Susan Welch, Michael Combs, and John Gruhl explore the question, "Do Black Judges Make a Difference?" They examine the factors that affect trial judges' sentencing decisions. The authors wanted to know whether white judges treat criminal defendants differently than black judges. The research question here is straightforward: Do sentencing decisions depend upon a judge's race?

Previous research was inconclusive—different studies found contradictory results. The authors noticed that earlier researchers failed to control for such important independent variables as the *severity of the defendent's crime*, the *defendant's previous record,* and other characteristics of the judge (such as *gender*).

Welch et al. develop their data from a sample of male defendants convicted of felonies between 1968 and 1979 in a large northeastern city. In one part of the analysis, they operationalize their dependent variable as the severity of the judge's sentence. They use a severity scale where 0 equals a suspended sentence; lower scores reflect fines and probation; higher scores reflect jail time; and the highest value, 93, equals life imprisonment. Because they wanted to control for multiple independent variables, they used multiple regression analysis.

Using a form of bivariate regression, they find that the judge's race (the independent variable) is *not* associated with sentence severity. That is, when they look only at the relationship between the judge's race and the severity of sentence, there is no relationship.[15] But when multiple regression is used and they introduce controls for severity of the defendant's crime and other factors, they find a significant, albeit slight, difference.[16] Black judges are associated with a sentence that is 1.22 units lower on the severity scale 0 to 93. This effect is particularly evident when the sample examined is limited to black defendants. Compared to white judges, black judges' sentences of black defendants are exactly two units lower in severity— however, there is more to the story.[17]

Probit Analysis

Welch and her colleagues also note that severity of sentencing is not the only aspect, or even the most critical aspect, of judicial sentencing decisions. Prior to deciding about the severity of the sentence, the judge must decide if the defendant will or will not be incarcerated. Some people are let off with probation, and although convicted of a felony, they are not required to spend time in jail.

When the dependent variable is conceived in these terms, regression analysis cannot be applied. Correlation and regression analysis assume that the dependent variable is measured at

---

[15]Beta $= -.01$, $b = -.48$; not significant.
[16]Beta $= -.03$, $b = -1.22$.
[17]Beta $= -.05$, $b = -2.00$.

the interval or ordinal level. *Decision to incarcerate,* however, is coded such that 1 = incarcerate, 0 = do not incarcerate. This being the case, we cannot talk about how a one unit change in the independent variable produces a change of some number of units in the dependent variable.

There is another form of analysis similar to multiple regression that is designed to deal with these dichotomous (two-category) dependent variables.[18] Social science researchers often deal with dependent variables that are simple nominal categories such as "yes or no" survey questions, or how various factors affect a government's decision to adopt a public policy or fight in a war. *Probit analysis* is being used with increasing frequency to address these questions.

Rather than producing regression coefficients or Betas, probit produces a coefficient that is not easily interpretable on its own. With the aid of a mathematical formula (omitted here for simplicity's sake), these coefficients can be used to assess how changes in X affect the *probability* that Y will assume one value or the other. This statistic can help answer the question as to whether a difference in the judge's race affects the probability that a felon will serve time in jail.[19]

Welch et al. use probit analysis to test the relationship between the independent variables and the decision to incarcer-

---

[18]The procedure is referred to as probit or logit analysis, or "logistic regression" in some cases. Probit and logit differ slightly in the assumptions made about the underlying distribution of the dependent variable. See J. Aldrich and F. Nelson, *Linear Probability, Logit and Probit Models,* Sage University Paper Series on Quantitative Applications in Social Science no. 45 (Beverly Hills, Calif.: 1984).

[19]When correlation and regression are used to test for a relationship, the statistics test how well the data are represented by a straight line or slope. When probit analysis is used, the statistic tests how well the relationship between X and Y is represented by an S-shaped curve. A statistic that searches for a linear association (correlation and regression) between the *decision to incarcerate* (Y) and the *severity of the crime* (X) might miss the relationship and lead to many errors in prediction.

ate.[20] They find that black judges are more likely to decide to incarcerate defendants than white judges. However, when the authors control for other variables, the significance of this effect disappears.

The probit analysis also shows that there are significant racial differences in the decision to incarcerate white defendants once controls for other factors are introduced into the analysis. White defendants are less likely to be sent to prison when sentenced by white judges; or, put differently, black judges are more likely to sentence white defendants to jail when severity of the crime and other factors are accounted for.

Welch and her colleagues conclude, after assessing all of the measures, that black judges do make a difference in the criminal justice system. Based upon the results of the multiple regression and probit analysis of this particular sample, black judges appear slightly more likely than white judges (1) to sentence white defendants to prison, and (2) to give slightly less severe sentences to black defendants. However, "in the decision about incarceration, black judges appear even-handed [as between black and white defendants], while white judges are less likely to send whites than blacks to jail."[21] Note that the authors qualify their results and make an effort to explain the multiple factors that might explain why blacks and whites behave differently.

As a way of summarizing what has been presented so far about measuring relationships between variables, see Table 5.8.

The central problem in regression has to do with sorting out the interrelated or statistically overlapping effects of several in-

---

[20]In Welch et al., Table 1, the probit coefficients are referred to as MLEs (maximum likelihood estimates). Welch et al. deem the coefficient significant if it is at least twice the size of its standard error (MLE/SE > 2.0).

[21]Appendix B.

TABLE 5.8   MEASUREMENTS OF RELATIONS BETWEEN
VARIABLES

Correlation:	The degree of association or covariation between two interval or ratio-level variables. Direction of the relationship is indicated by the plus or minus sign.
Bivariate regression:	The amount of change in an interval or ratio-level dependent variable associated with a one unit change in a single independent variable.
Multiple regression:	The amount of change in an interval or ratio-level dependent variable explained by several variables. Tests for the unique effect of each independent variable. Used in conjunction with R^2, which reports the proportion of variation in the dependent variable explained by the independent variables acting together.
Probit and logit analysis:	A form of multiple regression wherein the dependent variable is dichotomous (e.g., yes/no; for/against). Examines how a unit change in an independent variable will produce a change in the probability that the dependent variable will take one value or the other.

dependent variables on the dependent variable. The problem can be attacked, though rarely resolved completely, by precise operationalization, by analysis of the covariance of similar independent variables, and by such techniques as probit analysis.

In any multiple regression model or probit analysis, there are a good many technicalities, precautions, and limiting assumptions that need to be considered before the results are taken seriously. However, the logic of the analysis is what we are after here. Several variables affect judicial decisions. The researchers' logic suggests that some of these variables need to be accounted for, or controlled for statistically, in order that they might make conclusions about a variable they are particularly interested in: *race*. In the example, it appears that there are some significant effects of race, even after we control for other factors such as severity of the crime.

As technical as the statistics make it seem, regression and probit analysis, like science in general, begin with creativity and imagination. The first part of regression analysis involves figuring out which variables to test for—and this comes from an awareness of theory and a keen sense of the subject under investigation. The usefulness of regression analysis is that it indicates the possibilities for ever more precise measurement of relations between variables in hypotheses.

Computers and Statistics

The development of statistical software for computers makes it possible for researchers to process data quickly and efficiently. A certain amount of mathematical and conceptual background used to be the prerequisite for the calculation of statistics. Now computers can do the mathematics. In some instances, this means that data are manipulated in ways that are not appropriate to the level of measurement.

Although it is possible to leave the mathematics to a computer, it is dangerous to use statistical techniques without being fully aware of the conceptual foundations for mathematical processes. Just because a software package can produce a correlation statistic for two variables doesn't mean that the measurement standards necessary for correlation have been met. It is tempting to resort to software-produced statistics that seem to offer great precision; however, there is no substitute for a careful assessment of the properties and characteristics of the data according to the guidelines suggested here (see Figure 5.1).

Statistics don't create data; they describe it. Just as it would be nonsensical to describe something abstract by referring to its color or other physical properties, so is it misleading to claim statistical relationships where none can be calculated.

The refinements we have discussed are themselves just the beginnings of what can be done to elaborate and improve research strategies. We have sought only to map the major pathways of understanding and technique. Further development of research skills usually comes not so much from forced marches through methodology texts as from the motivation generated by an interesting project. As the project develops, methodological matters become more significant and more rewarding to learn.

In pursuing methodological understanding, however, beware of a simple "cookbook" approach. Understand the idea of what you are doing before enlisting the specific techniques by which it can be accomplished. That, at least, is the bias of this book and the experience of its authors. The wealth of detail found in the technical literature on methodology becomes much more digestible if the relatively simple ideas that underlie the calculations can be seen. Ideas provide frameworks for the mechanics of technique.

CONCEPTS INTRODUCED

Properties of variables
Measurement technique
Nominal
Ordinal
Interval
Ratio
True zero
Arbitrary zero
Probability
Level of significance
Probability sample
Stratification
Random sampling
Sample bias

Margin of error
Association
Descriptive statistics
Correlation
Direction of association
Scale of correlation
Contingency coefficient
Pearson's r
Regression analysis
Slope
Beta coefficient R and R^2
Multiple regression
Logit and probit analysis

QUESTIONS FOR DISCUSSION

1. Recall that samples are used to estimate something about a larger population. Considering this, how might the sampling technique and method used to gather the Perot data cause the results to be biased?

2. Examine the questions in Table 5.1 taken from the Perot survey. How might the wording of the questions introduce errors in measuring the attitudes of respondents?

3. Can you think of a more neutral wording for the Perot survey questions? How/why would neutral wording create a measure that better taps the attitudes of the population?

4. Is a baseball team's division finish (place in the division) an interval-level variable that taps the concept of *team performance* well? What would be a better interval-level measure of a team's performance?

5. Evaluate the conclusions that Welch et al. draw from their findings presented in Appendix B. Looking at their research design and the statistical results given in Table 1, can you tell what causes the relationship between the judge's race and the decision to incarcerate white defendants?
   a. Can you tell whether black judges are tougher on white defendants than are white judges?
   b. Can you tell whether white judges are simply more lenient toward white defendants than are black judges?

OUTLINE

CHAPTER SIX

REFLECTIONS: BACK TO THE ROOTS

"Knowledge joined to power represents nothing less than the history of life itself. . . ."

JOHN PATRICK DIGGINS

Our brief study began with the very foundations of knowing: the emergence of language concepts from elementary human experience. Now the structure of method raised on this foundation can, with the aid of insights gained by our look at the operational side of science, be addressed in a more sophisticated manner. It is time to put science itself into the perspective of a broader understanding. We need to know a little more of how science fits within a larger perspective on knowledge, how scientists relate to science, and, finally, how each of us can use science as a means of increasing our ability to deal with our own environment.

Factuality, Reality, and Actuality

The scientific method often appears at first as a kind of narrow and restrictive way of reaching understanding. The demands for precision are rigorous, the statistics forbidding, and, all too often, the results difficult to read. At the same time, zealous defenders of science sometimes indiscreetly claim for science more than it can support as a strategy of knowledge. Feigning a mythical objectivity, they confuse the procedures of science for testing hypotheses with a claim to personal and professional immunity from bias and prejudice.

In trying to gain perspective on science, we can learn something from one of this century's major theorists of the human condition, Erik Erikson. In the course of his experience as a psychoanalyst, his research on various subcultures, and his extensive studies of crucial personalities in history, Erikson came to characterize understanding as multidimensional. Erikson distinguishes between three dimensions of our relationship to the world around us: *factuality, reality,* and *actuality.*[1] Science, as we will see, is involved with each of these dimensions.

Of the three, *factuality* fits most closely with the popular view of scientific methodology. *Factuality is that "universe of facts, data, and techniques that can be verified with the observational methods and the work techniques of the time."*[2]

Much of what we have been considering here deals with the effort to establish that elusive item of inquiry, the fact. Earlier we hinted at a personal dislike for the word "fact." By now, however, enough has been said to make it clear that facts

---

[1]See Erik Erikson, *Gandhi's Truth* (New York: Norton, 1969), p. 396; *Dimensions of a New Identity* (New York: Norton, 1974), pp. 33–34; and *Life History and the Historical Moment* (New York: Norton, 1975), pp. 103–104. Erikson's formulations of these concepts vary somewhat, and we have adapted them to suit the purposes of this exposition.

[2]Erikson, *Dimensions of a New Identity,* p. 33, italics ours.

are not to be confused with Truth. A fact is only as good as the means of verification used to establish it, as well as the frame of reference within which it acquires meaning. A great deal of science consists of using methodological advances to revise, modify, or even falsify "facts" and theories formerly "verified" by cruder or less sensitive techniques. By trying to verify observations systematically, we strengthen the bridge between our perceptions of the world and phenomena outside ourselves.

All the concern with thoughtful variable specification, precise measurement, and the cautious interpretation of results has to do both with developing data worthy of being called factual *and* with understanding the limits of such data. Although the factual view of the world seldom seems to have the glamour or subtlety of, say, the poetic view, we have tried to establish that it has a power and social utility of its own. Factuality is a necessary component of our world view, though the limitations on creating factual information, and the human characteristics we bring to the task, require a broader perspective on knowledge.

Reality, the second of the dimensions, or aspects, of understanding, is seemingly less concrete but perhaps intuitively quite simple. Our sense of what constitutes reality is not merely a summation of factuality. *What we know as reality is, rather, a perspective on factuality integrated by the sense in which we understand these things.* Given the limitations of fact-gathering technique, the pressures of the moment, and the unconscious elements in the background of our understanding, we have to be aware that no matter how hard we try, our understanding will never be exclusively factual. Nor need it be. Science is a discipline for finding and organizing evidence about what interests us. We then try to use that evidence to shape our view of reality. Consequently, we can legitimately ask of those who engage in science that they convey to us not just the "facts" but something of their sense of the realities reflected in their data.

137

A science that is to be social must engage in a kind of balancing act between the scientific principle that statements must be verified and, on the other hand, the social necessity for doing something about the crises of civilization. Verification of social theory often lags behind the necessities of social policy. In bringing together the verified and the speculative through an insightful sense of reality, we increase the possibility of an informed understanding of the world—and of our ability to change it. Developing this kind of approach to reality is no simple matter, nor can we say exactly how it comes about—except that personal commitment, experience, a willingness to suspend preconceived ideas, and good scientific procedure all play a part.

Factuality, the world of data and observation, and a sense of reality, the perspective in which we understand evidence, do not yet constitute the whole of knowledge. Erikson suggests a third dimension of existence, *actuality,* which for our purposes means *knowledge gained in and through action.*

Science creates an image of reflective inquiry, of the researcher observing phenomena to gather information and then retreating to some quiet place to assemble, digest, and characterize what can be known. Yet such a detached mode of understanding is not typical of most of us. Human beings are, it seems, more oriented to action than reflection. Actuality has something to do with how we act on (or transact between) the modes of our knowing and the occasions for behavior.

Erikson illustrates his concept of actuality by discussing his own experience as a psychoanalyst. Psychoanalysis is basically a creative form of behavioral inquiry. Erikson comments that therapy is never really a process by which a doctor prescribes some course of action to a patient, but rather a *mutual* exploration to which the psychoanalyst brings training and experience, and the patient a personal history, deep feelings, and capacities for insights and action. The psychoanalytic encounter matches *potentialities* between doctor and patient.

The same can be said for social scientific inquiry. The behavior we study does not simply lie there on a slide plate or bubble in a test tube; it is formed out of the same animating principles that move the researcher as a person. The best social scientists are those who become engaged by the behavior they study. They use rigorous analysis, but they also reach into action itself as a source of understanding.

Social scientists are very circumspect about the question of personal involvement in the behavior they study. The obvious reason is that disciplined thought can be hard enough to achieve, without intruding on the feelings evoked by becoming engaged. Yet all social inquiry consists of a personal transaction with something outside ourselves. As a personal stance, detachment has its disadvantages just as involvement does. Whatever strategy is adopted, good inquiry really calls for a very high level of consciousness. *The scientific method makes conscious and explicit that part of the transaction dealing with the verification of observations.* There is a similar need to be highly conscious of how one's own experience and personality enter into the task of understanding.[3]

Aside from forcing a recognition of the personal elements of inquiry, Erikson suggests that experiential involvement opens up potentialities for insight. Behavior is reflexive; it emerges through transactions with an environment. Understanding the transactions experienced in an environment requires a "feel" for what is human about behavior. Such understanding demands an appreciation of factuality and a perspective on reality, but also a sense of action and what it can reveal.

Lately there has been increasing interest in what are now

[3]Some classics of social science owe their particular value to the personal involvement of the authors in their subject matter—for example, Floyd Hunter, *Community Power Structure* (New York: Doubleday, 1963); Robert Lane, *Political Ideology: Why the American Common Man Believes What He Does* (New York: Free Press, 1962); C. Wright Mills, *The Power Elite* (New York: Oxford University Press, 1959); and William Whyte, *Street Corner Society* (Chicago: University of Chicago Press, 1943).

called "observational studies." These studies try to capture a much larger proportion of the reality that is being studied. Open-ended interviews, evocative descriptions of the surroundings, and direct reporting of personal experience characterize this approach. Behind the apparent storylike quality of observational studies is usually a thoughtful effort to test some theories and provide evidence for hypotheses. The science is not so much in variable specification and the measurement of relationships as in locating the crucial observations and drawing out their theoretical implications.[4]

Every student has gone through the process of learning something intellectually and then relearning it through experience. Science is recommended as the mode of knowing that will most benefit one's ability to establish facts, to understand the reality surrounding them, and to approach actuality with sensitivity.

Science is more an attitude and a set of general guidelines than a specific strategy. There are many possible research strategies for getting at the various levels of factuality, reality, and actuality. The choice of strategies is part of the challenge.[5]

---

[4]For some resources on these methods, see Herbert Blumer, ed., "The Methodological Position of Symbolic Interaction," *Symbolic Interactionism: Perspective and Method* (Englewood Cliffs, N.J.: Prentice-Hall, 1969), pp. 1–60; Howard S. Becker, "Problems of Inference and Proof in Participant Observation," *American Sociological Review* 23 (1958); George McCall, "The Problem of Indicators in Participant Observation Research," *Issues in Participant Observation*, eds. George McCall and J. L. Simmons (Reading, Mass.: Addison-Wesley, 1969), pp. 230–239; and John Lofland, *Analyzing Social Settings* (Belmont, Calif.: Wadsworth, 1973).

[5]Some sources that will help with the problem of choosing between research strategies are: Morris Zelditch, Jr., "Some Methodological Problems in Field Studies," *American Journal of Sociology* 67 (March 1962):566–76; and Donald Warwick, "Survey Research and Participant Observation: A Benefit-Cost Analysis," *Comparative Research Methods*, eds. Donald Warwick and Samuel Asherson (Englewood Cliffs, N.J.: Prentice-Hall, 1973), pp. 189–203; and Davydd Greenwood, William Foote Whyte, and Ira Harkevy, "Participatory Action Research in a Process and as a Goal," *Human Relations* 46, no. 2 (1993): 175–192.

Feminist scholars have developed new perspectives on social science methodology that open up a broader range of strategies for thinking about evidence. Drawing on studies that point to significant differences in the psychological development of women and men, these scholars suggest that female approaches to the relational character of human society need to be incorporated into social scientific research designs. Techniques that rigidly control the definition of data and establish boundaries for categorizing responses to surveys, for example, need to be supplemented by long interviews and other forms of qualitative evidence gathering. In this view, studies that evoke the interdependent nature of human relationships, whether through qualitative or quantitative observations, should become a significant part of any social scientific inquiry.[6]

Morality and the Limits of Science

As the preceding discussion suggests, science does not answer all questions, and the answers it does provide must be placed in the perspective of other forms of understanding. In other words, science has its limitations. It is time to make these limitations explicit.

A concern for moral values that allow human beings to coexist in a civilized and peaceful fashion requires that we accept limits on how social science research is carried on, and on what is done with the results. A regard for prudence as well as ethics requires that we limit the claims of scientific

---

[6]See Sandra Harding, *Feminism and Methodology* (Bloomington: Indiana University Press, 1987); and Carol Gilligan, *In a Different Voice: Psychological Theory and Women's Development* (Cambridge, Mass.: Harvard University Press, 1982). For an interesting example of the use of these ideas in research, see Rand and Dana Jack, *Moral Vision and Professional Decisions: The Changing Values of Women and Men Lawyers* (New York: Cambridge University Press, 1989).

knowledge in view of what it *cannot* demonstrate and that we acknowledge the possibility that other strategies of knowledge may provide better answers. Each of these topics is worth further examination.

Taking a scientific approach to human behavior involves two major kinds of moral issues. The manipulation of people in research projects can be very risky to the individuals involved, and the results of scientific research can be used to exploit rather than to benefit people.

A famous example of the moral difficulties of manipulating experimental subjects is the Milgram experiments on obedience to authority.[7] The experiments required volunteers, under the direction of "scientific researchers," to administer electric shocks to "students" in order to encourage them to learn material that they were studying. The volunteers were told that the experiment had to do with testing a method for teaching people certain kinds of material more effectively. But the real point of the experiment was to test people's obedience to authority figures, in this case social scientific researchers. Unbeknownst to the volunteers, the electric shocks were phony, and the behavior of the volunteers themselves was the real subject of the experiment. There was a lot of deception involved here. The experiment was later explained to the volunteers and some were provided with follow-up counseling. A number of the volunteers were deeply upset to find that they had been willing to administer ostensibly dangerous electrical shocks to people in a blind response to professional authority.

Wrap the flag around an overzealous scientist and there is the possibility of a real disaster. The use of unsuspecting human subjects in determining the effects of radiation from nuclear

---

[7]Stanley Milgram, *The Individual in a Social World* (Reading, Mass.: Addison-Wesley, 1977).

emissions and bomb tests is a case in point. The U.S. government is now attempting to find out who was harmed and how they can be compensated.

The purpose of social science should be to improve the quality of human life. That noble end does not justify the use of means that degrade human life, either by deceiving people into doing something they would seriously regret under normal circumstances, or by exposing their inner motivations without taking responsibility for the results to the individual. Social scientists must be truthful with the subjects of experiments and obtain their informed consent as a condition of participation.

While the ethics of dealing with experimental subjects is a matter under the control and responsibility of the researcher, a much more difficult moral problem arises when we consider the exploitative potential of social science research. The debate over the uses of social science takes place in the shadow of the controversy concerning those scientists who did the original research for atomic weapons in the 1940s. Their argument was that they were pursuing the path of science—the *uses* of science being the province of others. Although social scientists have no atomic bombs to show for their efforts, the technology of social control that social science has begun to generate may well come to have a power of a magnitude worthy of the same moral concern.

We can't resolve these moral debates here, except to suggest that the cause of advancing science has no special ethical standing. To do something in the name of science doesn't excuse anybody from the moral considerations that make humane living possible.

The moral considerations discussed here do limit the kind of research that can be done in good conscience. Another limitation comes not from ethical considerations as applied to science but from the very nature of science itself. Remember that science begins—and also ends—in uncer-

143

tainty.[8] What science does is *reduce* uncertainty, but ultimately it cannot *eliminate* it. Were this possible, scientists would be gods rather than humans.

People disagree whether there are gods, and science can't settle the issue. The scientific method is merely a tool humans can use to try to reduce the inevitable uncertainty with which we all live. Humans are themselves observers of limited capacity, and the techniques and tools that science uses are imperfect. That is the reason for the emphasis on explicit evidence and the replication of findings.

The point is that true scientists generalize where there is evidence, but they do not claim more than the evidence allows. They certainly do not deny the possibility that other forms of knowledge (e.g., faith, intuition, or custom) may embody wisdom beyond the reach of evidence as scientists understand it. Scientists can and should use techniques of evidence to test the claims made by these other forms of knowledge. There are good results to show for the effort, as any inspection of medical history, for example, will demonstrate. Yet there remain medical results that are inexplicable by science. That these results may be attributable to forces beyond human comprehension can be doubted by anyone, but it cannot be denied in the name of science. Nor should claims based on faith be used to justify intolerance of what science has to offer.

To bring the point closer to social science, consider the uses and limits of the science of psychoanalysis. We know there are certain patterns of injurious behavior in adults that can be traced to traumas suffered at an early age, but that does not mean that all behavior originates in childhood experiences.

---

[8]It is possible to carry this point too far. After hearing a presentation on how physicists acknowledge that the nature of the universe is ultimately uncertain, a friend of one of the authors observed, "When those folks want to blow something up, they seem mighty certain about how to do it!"

There are clearly other forces at work. Sigmund Freud, the founder of modern psychoanalysis, once remarked that about a third of his patients got better, a third stayed the same, and a third got worse. Not bad, since he may have improved the odds for the first third; but this is nowhere close to the kind of result that a therapy based on perfect understanding would produce.

Consequently, psychoanalysis may be useful to some people in solving their problems, but it isn't an excuse for denying the possibility that there are alternative explanations for behavior—not until the evidence is much more precise. And even then, in this most human use of science, our very limitations as observers cannot lead to a claim of certainty for psychoanalysis—or any other science. Even the physical sciences operate in a cosmos surrounded by an infinity that defies measurement.

The message here is that a moral concern for humane values requires that there be a limit to both the arrogance of science as well as the claims of faith, intuition, and custom. If we are to deal with uncertainty effectively, a margin of tolerance for alternative forms of understanding is essential. Without it, we are likely to transcend the boundaries set by our human qualities. The results can be dangerous, as any number of religious executions, political massacres, and "scientifically" justified abuses of people's lives will testify.

Science is not a moral system. It is a strategy for learning about life and the universe—that and no more. Establishing the limits of faith, intuition, and custom is beyond the scope of this book, though our inquiry does suggest that all forms of knowledge should attempt to cohabit in the interests of civilized living.

Apart from understanding where science leaves off and faith begins, it is important to be aware that there are other approaches to knowledge besides science and religion. Science confines itself to the observable and to what we have termed "reality testing." In this respect social scientists follow natural scientists, who build up generalizations about observable evidence. Yet the behavior of human beings differs from plants and rocks in that it may be driven by nonobservable forces and designs.

As an example, the ancient Greek philosopher Plato thought that what we see as "reality" is merely appearance—an appearance that is in the process of moving toward, or away from, some perfect ideal that is hidden from view. Thus, every particular chair that we see is but an imperfect realization of an ideal chair that exists only in human imagination. Similarly, any existing form of government is an approximation to an ideal form of government that can be derived from an understanding of the human condition. This changes the meaning of knowledge. In Plato's view, to "know" about the government of, say, Chicago is to see where it fits in relation to an ideal typology of governments. By comparison with this typology, the successes and failures of Chicago's government can be defined, and predictions can be made about its future performance.

As another example, Karl Marx confuses most scientifically oriented readers by seeming to offer many definitions for such key concepts as class, alienation, and exploitation. Yet all his definitions fit within a dynamic model of a species struggling through various forms of historical development to realize its inner nature.

What is the inner nature of the human species? Marx approaches this question by distinguishing human beings from animals. What we have that they don't is the ability to choose what we produce. Animals produce hives and nests, for example, but they do it either by instinct or by accidental trial and error. Human beings, on the other hand, can take some twigs and make a nest, a boat, or some toothpicks. Marx believes that our species will become truly human when everyone spends a minimum of time producing for necessity, and a maximum of time in consciously chosen productive activity.

For Marx, then, exploitation is defined by the different ways that classes of people have used each other in various historical periods to secure necessities and achieve a measure of independence. The end of exploitation is a society in which all individuals will share the burden of necessary production so that all may share the freedom of consciously chosen productive activity. It is to be a society in which there are no classes, no alienation, and no domination.

The forms of knowledge Plato and Marx developed are, in one sense, beyond the realm of science, since they rely on "essences" and "intrinsic relations" that cannot be observed directly. In another sense, the observable aspects of the predictions that Plato's system allows, or of the historical patterns that Marx identifies, can be examined by using scientific approaches that may shed light on their usefulness as explanations of what is observed.

It is also possible to enter the methodological world of Plato or Marx and challenge the fundamental assumptions about these essences and relations—or the adequacy of Marx's view of our "species-nature."[9] The point is that human beings have the capacity to think beyond what *is* to what *might be,* or even to what *ought to be.* Prudence tells us that we need the best of all worlds of knowledge, not just the perfection of one of them.

Of Scientists, Science, and Paradigms

Science is practiced by people, not machines. Or, more accurately, science is practiced by groups of people. The major fields of social scientific inquiry are dominated by communities

---

[9]For further exploration of these ideas, see Kenneth Hoover, *Ideology and Political Life,* 2d ed. (Monterey, Calif.: Brooks/Cole, Inc., 1994), ch. 6. Cf. Bertell Ollman, *Alienation: Marx's Theory of Human Nature,* 2d ed. (New York: Cambridge University Press, 1976); Paul Thomas, "Marx and Science," *Political Studies* 24, no. 1 (1978):1–23; Terence Ball and James Farr, eds., *After Marx* (Cambridge: Cambridge University Press, 1984), pp. 217–260; and James Farr, "Marx's Laws," *Political Studies* 34, no. 2 (1986): 202–222.

of scientists, usually located at major research institutions, and tied together by a network of journals, conferences, and procedures for mutual evaluation and discussion.[10] Although substantial disagreements often exist within these scholarly communities, there is usually a rough consensus about the boundaries of the principal problems, the standards for dealing with them, and the values that must inform the recommendations. No one in the American social scientific community, for example, writes about the desirability of dictatorial government. And for a long time very few American scholars would consider seriously an openly Marxist approach to the understanding of social and political conflict.

The fact that there are communities of people involved in the enterprise of social science introduces a number of considerations that need to be reckoned with in evaluating social scientific research. First of all, few of us really like being unique or different from everyone else. Nor do people particularly enjoy having to face large problems from a point of view entirely their own. By this we mean that there is a natural psychological pressure toward conformity in all human activity, as well as in scientific inquiry.

Several factors reinforce this tendency toward conformity. One such factor is the career structure of academic disciplines. Though invisible to most students, careers in academic institutions typically hinge on a kind of master-apprentice system. Those who study with the famous master receive the best positions and the greatest access to means of communicating their views. Ability assuredly has a great deal to do with who gets close to the master and how successfully he or she

---

[10]An intriguing discussion of the history of science that details the role of scientific communities in structuring understanding is Thomas Kuhn's *The Structure of Scientific Revolutions*, 2d ed. (Chicago: University of Chicago Press, 1970), on which some of these themes are based.

manages to develop this position into a reputable scholarly career. But the net effect of this system is a significant pressure for the perpetuation of established viewpoints, since the apprentice frequently identifies with the position of his or her master.

To this pressure for conformity, add yet another factor: the political significance of social scientific research. Researchers who probe elements of corruption in the economic system or in social welfare agencies, for example, are not likely to enjoy the favor of their targets. Even the investigation of socioeconomic power as it enters into community decision making quickly becomes controversial. Since schools and institutions are usually run by trustees who represent dominant interests, there can be career risks in certain kinds of research projects.

Another factor influencing conformity with safer forms of social explanation is that research costs money. Survey research, upon which much good social science depends, costs a lot of money and usually requires financing from governmental agencies, businesses, or foundations. The kind of professional who attracts this money is not likely to be too far out of touch with prevailing social and political ideas.

For these reasons, scientific inquiry is frequently characterized by schools of thought or paradigms that structure the way in which problems are defined and solved. Yet in the face of all these pressures, the ultimate virtue of the scientific method, as opposed to other forms of inquiry, is that the steps by which knowledge is gathered are public and open to inspection and challenge. The point of reciting the factors that prejudice inquiry is not to discredit science, since most of these factors operate in other forms of inquiry as well, but rather to emphasize yet another reason for being critical of accepted knowledge and for being scientific in your own standards of evaluation. One of the first questions to ask when reading any book, taking any course, or selecting any field of research should be: What is the dominant paradigm behind this form of inquiry? Once that paradigm is understood, you are in a position to evaluate evidence carefully.

Making Social Science Serve Human Needs

For all its usefulness as a tool of inquiry, social science, as we have seen, also carries within its methodology a potential for domination and manipulation. Typically, the researcher uses data about human behavior to answer the questions of the researcher, rather than those that the subject of the experiment may need to have answered. The design of the inquiry may turn the subject into a passive respondent, whose behavior is being interpreted or redefined in a manner that is out of the subject's control. Finally, the purposes for which the research is used may rest on the priorities of those who have power over others, whether or not that power is being used for legitimate ends in the service of human needs.

An interesting approach to these problems, and to some of the limitations of social scientific methodology we have described here, has been developed by William Foote Whyte, Davydd Greenwood, Peter Lazes, and their associates at Cornell University.[11] Termed *participatory action research*, this technique retains the spirit of social scientific inquiry while opening up the process in ways that expand its usefulness to people and generate creative solutions to problems. Two examples illustrate how the technique can be used.

The Xerox Corporation, inventor of modern copiers, was for a time threatened by a drastic loss of market share due to

[11]Reported in William Foote Whyte, Davydd J. Greenwood, and Peter Lazes, "Participatory Action Research: Through Practice to Science in Social Research," *American Behavioral Scientists* 32, no. 5 (May/June 1989):513–551.

Japanese competition. The initial corporate response was to consider reducing labor costs by moving production jobs to nonunion areas. The focus of their analysis was on labor cost as the key variable, and the solution was simple: cut jobs and reduce wages. One researcher, called in to assist with this problem, suggested that the larger issue was the overall cost of production, not just direct labor, which accounted for less than 20 percent of the production cost, and that the workers themselves might have a few ideas about how to address it. By forming a "cost study team" with participation by researchers, union members, and management, the company identified a wide range of options. One of the more dramatic of these involved changing the ratio of indirect (nonproduction) employees to direct production workers from 2.1 to 1 in 1979 to .4 to 1 in 1985, while doubling total output. This was accomplished principally by shifting supervision and control functions to the workers themselves, while changing union rules to provide greater continuity of employment in various specializations.[12]

What is interesting from a methodological point of view is that the involvement of the "subjects" of the inquiry changed the definition of the key variables and the range of independent variables under consideration. Rather than just focusing on wage rates paid to production workers, the cost study team looked at training, continuity of the work force, and the role of indirect employees. The result was that the needed savings were realized, and competitive pricing was restored.

A second illustration adds new dimensions to the discussion. William Foote Whyte and Kathleen Whyte became interested in a network of more than one hundred industrial coopera-

---

[12]Whyte, Greenwood, and Lazes, "Participatory Action Research . . . ," pp. 524–525.

tives centered on the town of Mondragón in northern Spain.[13] These cooperatives included one of Spain's largest appliance manufacturers, as well as makers of electronic components and a wide array of internationally competitive products. The Mondragón network of producer cooperatives had established its own banking system, research institute, and health care and educational systems. The Mondragón cooperatives had achieved international significance as a model of worker ownership and control at a highly sophisticated level of production.

One classic problem faced by cooperatives is reconciling productive efficiency with significant levels of worker/owner participation. The question was how to analyze this problem so as to both enable Mondragón to succeed and allow for the kind of learning that would be transferable to other cooperative initiatives. A standard social scientific approach to measure participation would involve surveys of opinion about participation, together with analyses of instances of shared decision making. Based on these observations, generalizations could be developed about successful forms of participation.

The Whytes and their colleagues used this sort of research, but they put it together with a process of consultation and discussion that involved roundtables of cooperative worker/owners from various levels of the organization. Because the roundtables were asked not just to report on participation but to suggest ways of improving participation, previously unsuspected dimensions of participation were revealed and new variables could be conceptualized and measured. The "subjects" of the study became participants in the design of the research.

---

[13]See their *Making Mondragón: The Growth and Dynamics of the Worker Cooperative Complex* (Ithaca, N.Y.: Cornell University ILR Press, 1989). Cf. Kenneth Hoover, review of *Making Mondragón* in *American Political Science Review* 84, no. 1 (March 1990):351–352; and "Mondragón's Answers to Utopia's Problems," *Utopian Studies* 3, no. 2 (Summer 1992): 1–20.

These researchers were led to realize all the more force-fully that ". . . measurement is driven by definitions. Poor defi-nitions generate misleading measurements, which, added to-gether, yield misleading conclusions."[14] By broadening the sources as well as the purposes of definitions, these researchers gained new insight into worker participation, in one case, and corporate management in another. In the Xerox example, they came to realize that what was at issue was far more than *worker productivity;* the question was *organizational performance* in a complex international environment. By working toward conti-nuity of employment and increasing worker involvement in decision making, the overall performance of Xerox as a competi-tor was improved.

Note that the focus is on analysis directed toward *action* rather than just abstract understanding. This sort of inquiry is often referred to as "applied research," which is thought to be the poorer cousin of "pure research"—meaning research de-voted solely to intellectual questions. The point here is that in these cases, research applied to action yielded conceptualiza-tions and results that a "pure" researcher might never have obtained. As the authors of this approach point out:

> Rethinking past practice leads to theoretical reformula-
> tion that in turn leads to improved practice. The pro-
> cesses of rethinking both theory and practice thus
> strengthen both theory and practice.[15]

Participatory action research has the effect of bringing into play all three levels of analysis discussed earlier in this chapter: *factuality, reality, and actuality.* The result in both cases is that this form of research has now been incorporated

---

[14]Whyte, Greenwood, and Lazes, "Participatory Action Research . . . ," p. 548.
[15]Whyte, Greenwood, and Lazes, "Participatory Action Research . . . ," p. 540.

into the organizations themselves as a means of adapting to changing circumstances.

It may be a while before you are called in by Xerox to reorganize the company or asked to travel to Spain to investigate cooperatives; but this style of research has useful applications, whether you are studying participation in student elections, the responses of people to political advertising, or the sense of class and status that people live with in the workplace.

The Radicalism of Science

After what has been said about the conformist tendencies of the scientific establishment, even allowing for the brief message of reconsideration at the end, it may seem perverse to start talking about the radicalism of science. So be it; not all has yet been said on the subject. Science can be radical in a social sense and a personal sense as well.

Scientific inquiry began as a revolt against dogma established and controlled by dominant political and religious institutions. The history of science contains some important cases of intrepid analysts who emerged from their laboratories with findings that threatened prevailing understandings in various fields of human inquiry. Some scientists have paid even with their lives for such heresies. After all, the control of information is one of the fundamentals of political power. Scientists who insist on open and accountable procedures of information gathering and conclusion formation chip away at the power of those who would foreclose inquiry in favor of pet theories and self-serving ideologies and doctrines.

More relevant to daily life are the ways in which a scientific habit of mind can contribute to your own ability to resist conditioning and to deal knowledgeably with your environment. We are all bombarded with arguments to do this or that based on somebody else's conception of what is good and bad. For most people most of the time, estimations of the credibility of sources suffice to separate the smart advice from the nonsense. But it doesn't hurt to have a means of independent evaluation.

Western culture has for a long time viewed social problems as a matter of the weakness of human nature. This approach invites introspection and the examination of personal intentions, motives, and dispositions. Social science, by and large, encourages a different approach: Look around you. Before deciding that the individual is totally responsible for his or her actions, consider the environmental factors, the structures of power, the forces of conditioning, the real dimensions of choice that face people in social situations, and the material possibilities people actually have of solving their own problems. These circumstances are sometimes more susceptible to change than are inward dispositions that grow out of heredity as well as a conscious and unconscious history of individual development.

Science enters into personal action as a method for disciplining the process of understanding experience. The safeguards of the scientific method exist principally to control the natural tendency to project on what is observed whatever we want the world to be for our own private purposes. A discipline it is, but it becomes in practice a method of personal liberation from the narrowness of our own views, the limits of our own powers of observation, and the pressures of our prejudices. Science, a discipline all may develop, can become a radical force in a world that badly needs to be changed.

Science and Politics

There is no shortage of well-meant ideas for improving society. What is more often missing is a good method. Imposing utopia through the state, as Marxist-Leninists tried to do, or leaving its arrival to the voluntary action of self-interested individuals carries great hazards. Basic human rights are the first casualty of the statist method, and the loss of community values is frequently the result of the second. Well-informed and disciplined understanding can help avoid the worst excesses of both methods and establish the basis for interpersonal agreement without the use of coercion or the selfish assertion of one interest over another.

A trenchant observer of politics commented recently that:

> If political developments depended upon factual observations, false meanings would be discredited in time and a consensus upon valid ones would emerge, at least among informed and educated observers. That does not happen, even over long time periods. The characteristic of problems, leaders, and enemies that makes them political is precisely that controversy over their meanings is not resolved. . . . There is no politics respecting matters that evoke a consensus about the pertinent facts, their meanings, and the rational course of action.[16]

Without conceding all that may be implied in this critique of politics, the statement can be turned around. *To the extent that social issues can be dealt with on the basis of reliable information, the potential for conflict resolution is much higher.* Methodological discipline is a means of minimizing the distortion of information while maximizing the opportunities for mutual understanding.

There remain, of course, those essentially contestable issues over which agreement is much harder to reach, if not impossible.[17] Citizens and political leaders, unlike most scientists, are faced with the necessity for action. In the most constructive uses of politics, people achieve new insights and find shared interests

---

[16]Murray Edelman, *Constructing the Political Spectacle* (Chicago: University of Chicago Press, 1988), pp. 2–3.

[17]For an interesting exploration of "essentially contestable concepts" and their meaning for politics, see William Connolly, *The Terms of Political Discourse,* 2d ed. (Princeton, N.J.: Princeton University Press, 1983).

that yield effective forms of community action. The methods described in this book, practiced in a democratic context, can help that to happen, as they did in the Xerox and Mondragón examples. The realm of politics can include the honest search for truth by social scientific methods and other strategies as well, even though some differences must ultimately be resolved through political decision-making processes.

There is another potential in politics. It relies on the orchestration of meaning through symbolic appeals, and on the skillful use of threats and reassurances to mobilize support and induce quiescence among the possible opposition.[18] At the core of this kind of politics is the manipulation of information and, with it, of people. On the other hand, science deals with information in ways that can improve politics. A much-respected teacher once observed that "science is a way of organizing evidence—one that requires a social process of decision making that guards against rule by the few, as well as rule by the ignorant."[19]

Science and politics are both about the resolution of uncertainties, and both involve the demonstration of the truth. It was, after all, Mahatma Gandhi who brought down British colonial rule in India by a political technique he called *truth-force* (*satyagraha*). Gandhi organized protests that made clear the exploitative nature of British colonial rule. The British, once exposed to the pressure of world public opinion as well as to the concerted action of a newly mobilized populace, were forced to acquiesce.[20] The leaders of the American civil rights move-

[18]For examples, see Edelman, *Constructing the Political Spectacle,* chs. 3, 4, 5.

[19]The reference is to Aage Clausen, who has given invaluable advice on each edition of this book.

[20]For an analysis of the dynamics of *truth-force,* see Erik Erikson, *Gandhi's Truth* (New York: Norton, 1969). The discussion of *factuality, reality,* and *actuality* earlier in the chapter was drawn from Erikson's examination of Gandhi's technique. See specif. p. 396. Cf. Robert Coles, *Erik H. Erikson: The Growth of His Work* (New York: Norton, 1970), pp. 267–399.

ment, many of whom studied Gandhi's technique, did the same in confronting legal segregation in the United States.[21] The truth of exploitation and domination, once made clear through analysis and demonstration, turns out to be more powerful than manipulation, deceit, and coercion itself.

Ultimately, both truth-force and social scientific methodology depend upon a moral commitment to the values of honesty and integrity. The attempt to confront error and misunderstanding, to be credible, must rest on the search for truth. Without such a commitment, political action is dangerous and science is a fraud.

CONCEPTS INTRODUCED

Factuality

Reality

Actuality

Observational studies

Scientific communities

Career structures

Conformist social explanation

Participatory action research

Scientific radicalism

Conflict resolution through
   science

---

[21]Steven Oates, in his biography *Let the Trumpet Sound: The Life of Martin Luther King, Jr.* (New York: Harper and Row, 1982), reviews the development of King's approach to political leadership.

APPENDIX A

SCHEMATIC ASSESSMENTS OF
PRESIDENTIAL CANDIDATES*

ARTHUR H. MILLER
University of Iowa

MARTIN P. WATTENBERG
University of California, Irvine

OKSANA MALANCHUK
Frank N. Magid Associates
Marion, Iowa

This article applies theories of social cognition in an investigation of the dimensions of the assessments of candidates employed by voters

*Appendix A is an edited version of an article in the *American Political Science Review* 80, no. 2 (June 1986): 521–24. Reprinted with the permission of the *American Political Science Review.*

in the United States. An empirical description of the public's cognitive representations of presidential candidates, derived from responses to open-ended questions in the American National Election Studies from 1952 to 1984, reveals that perceptions of candidates are generally focused on "personality" characteristics rather than on issue concerns or partisan group connections. Contrary to the implications of past research, higher education is found to be correlated with a great likelihood of using personality categories rather than with making issue statements. While previous models have interpreted voting on the basis of candidate personality as indicative of superficial and idiosyncratic assessments, the data examined here indicate that they predominately reflect performance-relevant criteria such as competence, integrity, and reliability. In addition, both panel and aggregate time series data suggest that the categories that voters have used in the past influence how they will perceive future candidates, implying the application of schematic judgments. The reinterpretation presented here argues that these judgments reflect a rich cognitive representation of the candidates from which instrumental inferences are made.

Candidate evaluations are one of the most important but least understood facets of American voting behavior. In a classic article, Stokes (1966) argued that "personality" characteristics, rather than issues or parties, provide the best explanation for shifts in the vote from one presidential election to the next. Moreover, subsequent research has shown that candidates have been more salient to voters than political parties since the late fifties (Kagay and Caldeira, 1975; Miller, Miller, and Schneider, 1980), and that since 1956 candidate affect has been more directly related to the vote than party attachment (Kelley and Mirer, 1974; Markus and Converse, 1979; Miller and Miller, 1976).

Yet despite the unquestioned importance of candidate evaluations, systematic theoretical and empirical research has lagged far behind that devoted to parties and issues. This may in part reflect a predominate concern among social scientists for examining rational choice theories of candidate selection. Voting on the basis of personality characteristics is often viewed in the literature as "irrational" (cf. Converse, 1964; Page, 1978). The popular cynical view of candidates is that they are attractively packaged commoditiess devised by image makers who manipulate the public's perceptions by emphasizing traits with special appeal to the voting audience. Voters' judgments about alternative candidates are in this view based on superficial criteria such as the candidate's style or looks. . . .

Recently, a very different approach to candidate assessments has begun to appear in the literature. This emerging theory holds that candidate evaluations are not necessarily superficial, irrational, or purely short-term. Voters may focus on the personal qualities of a candidate to gain important information about characteristics relevant to assessing how the individual will perform in office (Kinder and Abelson, 1981; Popkin, Gorman, Phillips, and Smith, 1976; Shabad and Andersen, 1979). A similar perspective rooted in social psychological theory contends that criteria used in judging candidates reflects relatively general and enduring tendencies (Conover, 1981; Kinder, Peters, Abelson, and Fiske, 1980).

This new approach is largely based on the premise that individuals organize their thoughts about other people into broad preexisting categores. These category "prototypes" are then used in making judgments when only limited factual information is available (Cantor and Mischel, 1979). Kinder et al. (1980), for example, explore the features that may define an ideal president, to determine if people use this prototype to evaluate presidential candidates. They find that people can choose attributes they believe would make for an ideal president, but that these prototypic conceptions are related only to ratings of the incumbent president. In contrast, Foti, Fraser, and Lord (1982) demonstrate that preexisting cognitions about political roles are related to impressions of political leaders. Yet they only demonstrate the use of category labels such as "effective political leader" on two national figures, one of whom was president at the time of their study.

These results seem to support the traditional interpretation of candidate assessments as short-term indicators of electoral change. If the presidential prototype is primarily a reflection of characteristics associated with the incumbent, then the attributes describing an ideal president must be subject to considerable variation over time. However, given the timing of the Kinder et al. study (spring 1979), it is reasonable to assume that the situational context may not have provided sufficient cues to evoke prototypical cognitions about any potential candidate other than Carter, who was then the incumbent. In short, the evidence testing the question of whether voters judge actual candidates against some prototype remains inconclusive.

It is our contention that a presidential prototype, or *schema,* as we shall label it, can and will be evoked during the actual campaign period when people receive the appropriate stimuli to trigger these preexisting cognitions. . . .

Theoretical Predictions of Presidential Criteria

Current theories of social cognition posit that people deal with the flood of information in their environment by employing cognitive shortcuts (Nisbett and Ross, 1980). The basic assumption is that humans are active information processors and cognitive misers (Taylor and Crocker, 1981). This theory contends that people categorize objects and simplify information as a result of general limits to human cognitive capacity. The complexity of the real world becomes simplified in our minds through a dynamic process that combines experience with real-world occurrences (and co-occurrences of objects and events) and the results of active mental processes, including the inferences we make to fill in missing information or go beyond the information directly available to us (Fiske and Taylor, 1984). These mental representations of the world, frequently called *schemas,* function to direct our attention and aid in the storage and retrieval of information in a manner than influences both our memory of previous experience and the acquisition of new information (Fiske and Linville, 1980; Taylor and Crocker, 1981).

What this theory suggests for our purposes is that voters do not evaluate each political contender *de novo,* or simply with respect to readily apparent attributes, but rather in terms of their own embellished perceptions. As Lippman (1922) noted, "We do not so much see this man and that sunset; rather we notice the thing is man or sunset and then see chiefly what our mind is already full of on those subjects."

Person schemas are knowledge structures about people, and schemata about political candidates are organized cognitions about them in their political role. Candidate schemas thus reduce the complexity of our impressions by enabling us to categorize and label an individual politician according to certain abstract or representative features. These categories then serve as a set of cues from which we can draw further inferences about the candidate's future behavior (Schneider, Hastorf, and Ellsworth, 1979). For example, labeling Walter Mondale as a "big spender" may cue other unstated or inferred properties among conservatives, such as being a weak leader, being overly sympathetic toward those on welfare, and, of course, being a liberal.

This process of schematic thinking about candidates is similar to overt stereotyping, in which one assigns unobservable dispositional qualities (e.g., attitudes or intentions) to another. It is usually initiated by some social or physical feature of the perceived individual, a distinctive biographical fact or observable behavior pattern, or some commonly recognized label such as "Democrat" or "liberal." Once invoked, it acts to embellish what we know about the person and provides an implicit cognitive theory regarding what we expect of the person in the future (Cantor and Mischel, 1979). Schematic images are abstracted from prior experience. Political candidates, especially those running for the presidency, would therefore appear to be prime targets for schematic thinking. Besides all the daily information about the incumbent president, people generally have observed enough presidential candidates that it seems reasonable to hypothesize that they will employ categorical criteria when evaluating them.

Another hypothesis suggested by this theoretical framework is that a few broad criteria, rather than specific information, will be used to judge candidates. Furthermore, these categories should be similar over time, despite the uniqueness of each candidate. We would also predict, for reasons spelled out below, that comments of a personal nature, rather than issues or partisan ties, should predominate in these evaluations. Contrary to the common assumption by those who view personality as irrational, schema theories suggest that more politically informed voters will be the most likely to make comments about the candidates' inner dispositions and behaviors. These types of assessment reflect inferences that go beyond the available information, and cognitive theories predict that people with "richer" schemas will make considerably more inferences, based on their larger store of

163

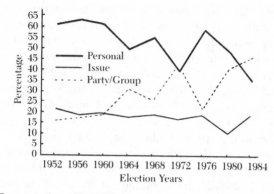

FIGURE 1   THE DISTRIBUTION OF PERSONAL,
ISSUE, AND PARTISAN COMMENTS ABOUT
PRESIDENTIAL CANDIDATES, 1952–1984

NOTE: Data are the percentage of all comments in all three dimensions. Comments associating candidates with particular groups were combined with those mentioning party connections. As party differences were frequently discussed in terms of the groups they usually benefit, the two sets of comments are theoretically similar.

SOURCE: SRC/CPS National Election Studies.

experience with the object. . . . In sum, the frequency with which particular attributes will be used in appraising presidential candidates should reflect the availability of informational cues, the personal relevance of these cues, and one's knowledge about politics.

Party, Issues, or Personality?

To examine the general framework people use in organizing their thinking about politics, it is important to ascertain how thoughts are structured. Because open-ended questions allow respondents to establish their own frame of reference, they are particularly well suited for this purpose. By examining the distributions and interrelationships among thousands of open-ended comments about the candidates obtained in the 1952–1984 NES studies, we can gain substantial clues about the cognitive representations people have of political leaders. The frequency of mentions will denote the relative importance of particular characteristics for the public; the way these comments are organized into larger domains (as determined via factor analysis) will reveal the basic structures underlying the multitude of responses. Fortunately, the relevant open-ended questions about candidates have been asked in exactly the same way since 1952, thus eliminating any methodological concerns about changes in the wording of questions. . . .

Cognitive Categories Underlying Personality Comments

Numerous statements have been made by survey respondents regarding the various candidates who have run for the presidency during the past quarter-century covered by the NES. The most crucial use of these data for our purposes is to determine if the comments cluster together into relatively few general categories, as schema theory would predict, and to ascertain from the content of the comments what judgmental criteria are employed. Previous researchers (Campbell, Gurin, and Miller, 1954; Page, 1978; Shabad and Andersen, 1979) have organized people's responses in a number of different fashions according to their own particular interests. The variation in the resulting categorization schemes suggests the need for a systematic, empirically based approach to these open-ended responses. Rather than imposing ad hoc typologies on people's comments, we have chosen to investigate empirically how the respondents themselves structure their responses.

The approach employed was to apply factor analysis to the set of comments made by the respondents.[1] In each of the years examined,

---

[1] The factor analysis proceeded by first forming a series of dummy variables for all the codes in the open-ended questions that deal with candidate attributes. The dummy variables were coded one if the respondent mentioned a particular candidate characteristic, and zero if no mention was made. A tetrachoric r correlation matrix was then computed for all the resulting dummy variables in the 1956, 1972, and 1976 surveys, and subjected to factor analysis using both orthogonal and oblique rotations. Selecting only those factors with eigenvalues greater than 1.0 produced a five-

the factor analysis showed a five-dimensional solution as the best fit to the data. Although the components are not perfectly distinct for every year, they are clearly separate—the average correlation among the factors was only .10. These results confirm the prediction from schema theory that people think about presidential candidates in terms of a limited number of broad categories rather than in terms of a multitude of discrete traits. While the categories are similar in some respects to those used by previous researchers, they have the advantage of being identified through an analysis of the data themselves rather than by preconceived notions of the investigator.

The first generic category or dimension people use involves the candidate's past political experience, ability as a statesman, comprehension of political issues, and intelligence; we call this *competence.* Another dimension, *integrity,* deals with notions of trustworthiness and includes remarks such as "honest," "sincere," and "just another politician," and references to corruption in government. A third dimension, *reliability,* is similar to integrity but contains important distinctions. Reliability refers to a candidate as dependable, strong, hardworking, decisive, aggressive, or the opposite of any of these. That the two dimensions are separate is most evident in the evaluations of Goldwater, who received the highest integrity rating of any candidate except Eisenhower and the lowest reliability rating of any candidate in the entire series. Reliability thus serves as a bridge between integrity and competence. Perhaps the best description of it would be trust in terms of capability rather than honesty.

---

dimensional solution that accounted for 68%, 65%, and 71% of the total item variance in 1956, 1972, and 1976, respectively.

The final solutions for each of the factor analyses were then compared to determine their degree of similarity. Using the OSIRIS COMPARE program with 1972 as the target configuration, measures of fit (normalized symmetric error ranging from .028 to .031) indicated that the three different solutions were virtually identical (Schonemann and Carroll, 1970). In addition, an examination of the correlations among the measures created to indicate each of the five dimensions suggested that the structure underlying the comments was similar in all three years. Given these comparisons, it was decided that further application of these techniques to the survey data for other years was not necessary. Please see the Appendix for information on the specific code categories incorporated into the measure for each of the five dimensions.

A fourth factor, which we label *charisma*, encompasses a candidate's leadership, dignity, humblenes, patriotism, and ability to get along with, communicate with, and inspire people. Finally, a fifth major category can be seen as comprising the most purely personal comments. Included here are references to a number of observable features about the candidates' appearance (e.g., age, health, smile, speech pattern) or background factors (e.g., military experience, religion, wealth, previous occupation). We refer to this as the *personal* dimension, but it should not be confused with the label *personal attributes* that has traditionally been used to designate all of the comments encompassed by the five different dimensions. (Please see the Appendix for a complete list of which codes fell onto which factors.)

In summary, the factor analysis demonstrates that people do in fact think about candidates in terms of a limited set of broad categories. These categories appear to incorporate both observable descriptive characteristics and inferred dispositions that citizens group in a coherent and consistent fashion when judging candidates. That most of the specific comments are incorporated by the five dimensions indicates rather widespread consensual cognitions of political candidates. . . .

The Prevalence of Specific Characteristics over Time

Further evidence relevant to the question of whether people use relatively stable judgmental categories to evaluate candidates comes from an examination of the frequency with which the various categories have been employed over time. Despite the uniqueness of each specific candidate, we can expect that the inherent nature of schematic structures will limit their accommodation to new information. The novelty of each candidate and the historical situation may influence the prevalence of different criteria, but continuity in the general dimensions used in judging presidential contenders across time would further confirm that people process information about candidates schematically.

Over the years, respondents have consistently made more com-

TABLE 1   THE RELATIVE PREVALENCE OF GENERIC
CATEGORIES OF CANDIDATE CHARACTERISTICS, 1952–1984

Dimension	1952	1956	1960	1964	1968	1972	1976	1980	1984
Competence	36	41	46	39	42	42	39	44	39
Integrity	14	15	9	18	16	25	27	16	16
Reliability	5	5	8	24	19	22	13	16	17
Charisma	10	9	6	8	9	5	5	5	10
Personal	35	30	31	11	14	6	16	19	18

NOTE: Table entries are percentages of all comments from the five dimensions.
SOURCE: National Election Studies, University of Michigan Center for Political Studies.

ments reflecting the internal dispositions and expected behaviors represented by the dimensions of competence, integrity, and reliability (see Table 1). Remarks concerning candidate competence have consistently been the most prevalent, thereby implying that voters are quite sensitive to cues concerning the candidate's past or potential performance in office. . . .

The Continuity of Judgmental Criteria

The endurance of these prototypical judgmental criteria suggested by the aggregate figures is further supported by panel data. Those respondents who used the competence, integrity, or reliability dimensions for evaluating a candidate at one point in time were significantly more likely to employ the same dimension four years later, even though different candidates were now running for office (see Table 2). For example, 70% of the 1956–60 panel respondents who mentioned competence in 1956 did so again in 1960, compared to only 45% for those who had not used competence in their evaluations in 1956. Similar differences were also generally found for the integrity and reliability categories in both the 1956–60 and 1972–76 panels.

The degree of continuity in the three main judgmental categories—competence, integrity, and reliability—when assessing candidates is significantly higher than might be expected given all the measurement problems involved in coding open-ended responses.

TABLE 2 STABILITY ACROSS TIME OF COGNITIVE
DIMENSIONS USED IN EVALUATING CANDIDATES, AS
DETERMINED FROM PANEL DATA

| | Percentage mentioning dimension in: | | | |
| | 1960 | | 1976 | |
Dimension	Who Used It in 1956	Who Did Not Use It in 1956	Who Used It in 1972	Who Did Not Use It in 1972
Competence	70	45	66	47
Integrity	49	23	59	38
Reliability	20	11	49	26
Charisma	38	20	21	16
Personal	52	41	35	33

SOURCE: National Panel Studies, University of Michigan Center for Political Studies.

This is not to imply, however, that the use of these criteria is unaffected by historical circumstances or the events of particular campaigns. On the contrary, the percentages for integrity and reliability in Table 2 reveal a general increase in these concerns during the 1970s, when citizens began to question whether politicians could and would do what they promised. Nevertheless, respondents who had employed one of the three major personal dimensions in the 1972 campaign were significantly more likely to use the very same criterion four years later when assessing two new candidates for the presidency. A much lower level of continuity was found for the dimensions of charisma and personal characteristics (see Table 2). Such instability further demonstrates the sensitivity of these two criteria to the unique features of specific candidates.[2] . . .

[2] A multivariate analysis with panel data confirms the results of Table 2. Mention of a dimension in 1972 was used to predict the use of the same dimension in 1976 after controlling for education, strength of party identification, and media usage. The results demonstrate that the prior use of the competence, integrity, and reliability dimensions significantly predicted (better than .001 level) the subsequent use of these dimensions, whereas no significant impact across time was found for the charisma or personal dimensions.

TABLE 3   AVERAGE NUMBER OF COMMENTS ON PERSONAL
ATTRIBUTE DIMENSIONS, BY LEVEL OF EDUCATION

Education	*Competence*	*Integrity*	*Reliability*	*Charisma*	*Personal*
Grade School	.58	.19	.19	.10	.37
High School	.76	.38	.29	.19	.47
College	1.15	.74	.66	.29	.48

NOTE: For the sake of parsimony the number of comments per dimension was averaged over the years 1952–1984 rather than presenting the figures for each year. Values for the individual years can be obtained by writing the authors.

SOURCE: National Election Studies, University of Michigan Center for Political Studies.

Explaining Candidate Assessment Dimensions

The consistent predominance of comments referring to competence, integrity, and reliability offers a considerably different interpretation regarding the meaning and political relevance of personality responses than is standard in the literature. The finding that better-educated people are more likely to offer personal comments now seems more understandable. As can be seen from Table 3, the competence, integrity, and reliability dimensions are those most frequently mentioned by better-educated respondents. There is only a slight tendency for well-educated people to make more comments pertaining to the charisma and personal dimensions, and within education levels it is clear that these features are more salient to those voters with the least education. Therefore, a partial explanation for the decline noted earlier across time in comments referring to personal attributes may be the general rise in education that occurred during this period.

In sum, college-educated voters appear more likely to make inferences about the expected performance and internal dispositions of the candidates, whereas less-educated voters rely on more readily observable features. These observable features of the presidential contenders should cue inferences about the expected behavior of candidates according to the social cognition theory outlined above. Unique aspects of the candidates' looks, behavioral mannerisms, and background are often quite vivid and well known, thus providing relatively cost-free information used by many voters when evaluating candidates (Her-

TABLE 4   MULTIPLE CORRELATION BETWEEN EVALUATIONS OF
PERSONAL CANDIDATE CHARACTERISTICS AND COMPETENCE,
INTEGRITY, RELIABILITY, AND CHARISMA, BY EDUCATION

Education	1952	1956	1960	1964	1968	1972	1976	1980	1984
Grade School	.30	.25	.24	.19	.25	.26	.35	.19	.21
High School	.18	.14	.19	.13	.18	.15	.16	.18	.19
College	.09	.13	.08	.11	.12	.14	.11	.20	.12

SOURCE: National Election Studies, University of Michigan Center for Political Studies

stein, 1981). Therefore, we would expect that personal characteristics should carry more weight in schematic judgments made by the least-informed voters.

The evidence presented in Table 4 does, in fact, suggest that people—especially those with a low level of education—draw inferences about the competence, integrity, reliability, and charisma of a candidate from the candidate's personal characteristics. . . .

Conclusion

The evidence presented above provides consistent support for the theory that Americans evaluate presidential candidates on the basis of a limited set of general and enduring criteria. In other words, people have a preexisting knowledge structure, or schema, concerning what a president should be like, and judge real candidates according to how well they match the elements of these schemas. While these criteria have remained quite stable over time, the relative importance of particular categories has varied with changes in historical circumstances. The primary dimension used by citizens throughout the 1952–1984 period has been competence, clearly a performance-related criteri[on]. Integrity and reliability have become more prevalent in judgments of candidates since 1964. These broad expectations that citizens hold about presidential performance appear to reflect in part the actions of past presidents and in part the agenda as set by the media or by current candidates.

The cognitive process underlying the evaluation of candidates, which we have described above, is clearly a dynamic one involving an interaction between the individual and the political environment. Voters abstract from their experience of past presidents those features and behaviors they associate with political success, and then evaluate other candidates with respect to these same characteristics. During the campaign the candidates no doubt emphasize certain characteristics in ways that reflect on or cue judgments of their competence, integrity, and reliability, because they believe these are relevant to the conduct of the office. Voters in turn respond to these campaign messages not only because they are relevant to their schema for presidential candidates, but also because these are the terms in which the political dialogue is conducted. Particular events of the campaign and the unique strengths and weaknesses of the specific candidates, as well as cognitive and personal variation across individual voters, focus attention on certain of these criteria, giving more emphasis to some and less to others. Nevertheless, despite some variation in the specific content of political cognitions across time, the general structure of the abstracted inferences and judgments derived from the historical particulars remains fairly stable over the years.[3] . . .

Evaluating candidates on the basis of personal qualities has for years been regarded as emotional, irrational, and lacking in political relevance. This interpretation arose in part because candidate evaluations were considered to be uninformed idiosyncratic responses based on superficial criteria. The evidence now suggests that a reinterpretation is clearly needed. Rather than represent a concern with appearance, candidate assessments actually concentrate on instrumen-

---

[3] Recent research has suggested that a new "compassion" or "empathy" dimension of candidate evaluations may be emerging since 1980 (Kinder, 1985). A close examination of the open-ended NES responses relevant to this theme, however, reveals little support for this contention. The percentage of comments that referred to codes encompassing compassion (codes 435, 436, 807, 808, 831, and 832) was only 3.3% in 1984, compared to 3% in 1980. Our analysis shows that closed-ended items that initially may be thought of as compassion, such as "in touch with ordinary people" or "really cares about people like me," are largely incorporated by the group benefits dimension in the open-ended responses.

tal concerns about the manner in which a candidate would conduct governmental affairs. In general, they represent a schematic conception of the president as someone who can be relied upon to deal competently with the nation's problems in an honest and even-handed manner.

Appendix

The following is a list of the codes from the National Election Studies (NES) which form each of the five personal dimensions for our baseline year of 1972. In earlier years some of the codes on different dimensions were combined, necessitating the reading of the actual protocols for these cases to sort out the various codes and maintain consistency from year to year.

Integrity

313. A politician/political person; (too) much in politics; a good politician
314. Not a politician; not in politics; above politics; a bad politician
401. Honest/sincere; keeps promises; man of integrity; means what he says; not tricky
402. Dishonest/insincere; breaks promises; no integrity; doesn't mean what he says; tricky
403. Man of high principles/ideals; high moral purpose; idealistic
404. Lacks principles/ideals; not idealistic
603. Honest government; not corrupt; no "mess in Washington"
604. Dishonest/corrupt government; "mess in Washington"

Reliability

213. Dependable/reliable; a man you can trust with the responsibilities of government ("trust" in the capability sense, rather than the honesty sense)
214. Undependable/unreliable; a man you can't trust with the responsibilities of government
319. (too) careful/cautious
320. (too) impulsive/careless
407. Public servant; man of duty; conscientious; hard-working; would be a full-time President
408. Does not take public service seriously; lazy; would be a part-time President
431. Unsafe/unstable; dictatorial; craves power
432. Safe/stable

709. Good for country; has country's best interests at heart
710. Bad for country; doesn't have country's best interests at heart

Competence

201. General reference to him as "a good/bad man"; R has heard good/bad things about him; qualifications; general ability (low priority code)
211. Experienced
212. Inexperienced
217. His record in public service; how well he's performed in previous offices
218. Has government experience/political experience
219. Lacks government experience/political experience
220. A statesman; has diplomatic experience
221. Not a statesman; lacks diplomatic experience
315. Independent; no one runs him; his own boss
316. Not independent; run by others; not his own man/boss
413. Understands the nation's problems; well-informed
414. Doesn't understand the nation's problems; poorly informed
415. Idealistic/pragmatic/practical; down-to-earth; not too idealistic
416. Too idealistic
417. Uses common sense; makes a lot of sense
418. Not sensible; impractical
419. (too) well educated; scholarly
420. Poorly educated; unschooled
421. Intelligent/smart
422. Unintelligent/stupid/dumb
601. Good/efficient/businesslike administration
602. Bad/inefficient/unbusinesslike administration
609. General assessment of job he would do; he'd be a good/bad President, provide good/bad administration (low priority code)
707. Candidate as good protector; will know what to do
708. Candidate as bad protector; won't know what to do

Charisma

301. Dignified/has dignity
302. Undignified/lacks dignity
305. Inspiring; a man you can follow; "a leader"
306. Uninspiring; not a man you can follow; not a leader
307. People have confidence in him
308. People don't have confidence in him
309. Good at communicating with blacks, young people, other "problem" groups

310. Bad at communicating with blacks, young people, other "problem" groups
311. Knows how to handle people (at personal level)
312. Doesn't know how to handle people (at personal level)
317. Humble; knows his limitations; doesn't pretend to know all the answers
318. Not humble enough; too cocky/self-confident
411. Patriotic
412. Unpatriotic
433. Sense of humor; jokes a lot/(too much)
434. No sense of humor/humorless/(too) serious
435. Kind/warm/gentle
436. Cold/aloof
437. Likeable/gets along with people
438. Unlikeable/can't get along with people
439. Democratic (in nonpartisan sense)
440. Undemocratic (in nonpartisan sense)
441. High-fallutin/high-brow; talks in circles; can't talk to common man; can't communicate ideas well
442. Not high-fallutin/low-brow; talks straight; can talk to common man
703. Will save America; America needs him
704. Will ruin America; last thing America needs
705. Will unite Americans/bring people together
706. Will divide Americans/drive people apart

Personal

215. A military man; a good military/war record
216. Not a military man; bad military/war record; no military/war record
423. Religious; "moral" (in religious sense); God-fearing
424. Irreligious; "immoral" (in religious sense)
425. Self-made; not well off; started out as a poor boy
426. Wealthy; rich; born with silver spoon in his mouth
443. Well-known
444. Unknown/not well-known
445. Reference to his family
446. Reference to his wife
447. His speaking ability
448. His health
449. His appearance/looks/face/appearance on TV
450. His age
451. (too) old
452. (too) young
453. Mature
454. Immature

Appendix A

References

Campbell, Angus, Philip E. Converse, Warren E. Miller, and Donald E. Stokes. 1960. *The American Voter*. New York: Wiley.

Campbell, Angus, Gerald Gurin, and Warren E. Miller. 1954. *The Voter Decides*. Evanston, IL: Row and Peterson.

Cantor, Nancy, and Walter Mischel. 1979. Prototypes in Person Perception. In Leonard Berkowitz, ed., *Advances in Experimental Social Psychology*, vol. 12. New York: Academic Press.

Conover, Pamela J. 1981. Political Cues and the Perception of Candidates. *American Politics Quarterly*, 9:427–48.

Converse, Philip E. 1964. The Nature of Belief Systems in Mass Publics. In David Apter, ed., *Ideology and Discontent*. New York: Free Press.

Downs, Anthony. 1957. *An Economic Theory of Democracy*. New York: Harper and Row.

Fiorina, Morris P. 1981. *Retrospective Voting in American National Elections*, New Haven: Yale University Press.

Fiske, Susan T. 1985. Schema-Based Versus Piecemeal Politics. In *Political Cognition*. *See* Lau and Sears, 1985.

Fiske, Susan T., and Patricia W. Linville. 1980. What Does the Schema Concept Buy Us? *Personality and Social Psychology Bulletin*, 6:543–57.

Fiske, Susan T., and Shelley E. Taylor. 1984. *Social Cognition*. Menlo Park, CA: Addison-Wesley.

Foti, Roseanne, Scott Fraser, and Robert Lord. 1982. Effects of Leadership Labels and Prototypes on Perceptions of Political Leaders. *Journal of Applied Psychology*, 67:326–33.

Graber, Doris A. 1976. Press and T.V. as Opinion Resources in Presidential Campaigns. *Public Opinion Quarterly*, 40:285–303.

Graber, Doris A. 1980. *Mass Media and American Politics*. Washington, D.C.: Congressional Quarterly Press.

Herstein, John A. 1981. Keeping the Voter's Limits in Mind: A Cognitive Process Analysis of Decision Making in Voting. *Journal of Personality and Social Psychology*, 40:843–61.

Kagay, Michael R., and Gregory A. Caldeira. 1975. I Like the Looks of His Face: Elements of Electoral Choice, 1952–1972. Presented at the annual meeting of the American Political Science Association, San Francisco.

Kelley, Stanley, and Thad Mirer. 1974. The Simple Act of Voting. *American Political Science Review*, 68:572–91.

Kiesler, Charles A., Barry E. Collins, and Norman Miller. 1969. *Attitude Change: A Critical Analysis of Theoretical Approaches*. New York: Wiley.

176

Kinder, Donald R. 1985. Presidential Character Revisited. In *Political Cognition. See* Lau and Sears, 1985.

Kinder, Donald R., and Robert P. Abelson. 1981. Appraising Presidential Candidates: Personality and Affect in the 1980 Campaign. Presented at the annual meeting of the American Political Science Association, New York.

Kinder, Donald R., Mark D. Peters, Robert P. Abelson, and Susan T. Fiske. 1980. Presidential Prototypes. *Political Behavior*, 2:315–37.

Lau, Richard R. 1985. Political Schemas, Candidate Evaluations and Voting Behavior. In *Political Cognition. See* Lau and Sears, 1985.

Lau, Richard R., and David O. Sears, eds. 1985. *Political Cognition.* Hillsdale, NJ: Lawrence Erlbaum Associates.

Lippman, Walter. 1922. *Public Opinion.* New York: Harcourt and Brace.

Markus, Hazel. 1977. Self-Schemata and Processing Information about the Self. *Journal of Personality and Social Psychology*, 35:63–78.

Markus, Gregory B., and Philip E. Converse. 1979. A Dynamic Simultaneous Equation Model of Electoral Choice. *American Political Science Review*, 73:1055–70.

Miller, Arthur H., and Michael MacKuen. 1979. Informing the Electorate: A National Study. In Sidney Kraus, ed., *The Great Debates: Carter vs. Ford 1976.* Bloomington: Indiana University Press.

Miller, Arthur H., and Warren E. Miller. 1976. Ideology in the 1972 Election: Myth or Reality? *American Political Science Review*, 70:832–49.

Miller, Arthur H., and Martin P. Wattenberg. 1981. Policy and Performance Voting in the 1980 Elections. Presented at the annual meeting of the American Political Science Association, New York.

Miller, Warren E., Arthur H. Miller, and Edward J. Schneider. 1980. *American National Election Studies Data Sourcebook, 1952–1978.* Cambridge, MA: Harvard University Press.

Nisbett, Richard E., and Lee Ross. 1980. *Human Inference: Strategies and Shortcomings in Social Judgments.* Englewood Cliffs, NJ: Prentice-Hall.

Page, Benjamin I. 1978. *Choices and Echoes in Presidential Elections.* Chicago: Chicago University Press.

Popkin, Samuel, John W. Gorman, Charles Phillips, and Jeffrey A. Smith. 1976. What Have You Done for Me Lately? Toward an Investment Theory of Voting. *American Political Science Review*, 70:779–805.

Rabinowitz, George. 1978. On the Nature of Political Issues: Insights from a Spatial Analysis. *American Journal of Political Science*, 22:793–817.

Rosenstone, Steven J., Roy L. Behr, and Edward H. Lazarus. 1984. *Third Parties in America: Citizen Response to Major Party Failure.* Princeton: Princeton University Press.

Rusk, Jerrold G., and Herbert F. Weinberg. 1972. Perceptions of Presidential Candidates: Implications for Electoral Change. *Midwest Journal of Political Science*, 16:388–410.

Sears, David O. 1969. Political Behavior. In Gardner Lindzey and Elliot Aronson, eds., *The Handbook of Social Psychology*, 2d ed., vol. 5. Reading, MA: Addison-Wesley.

Schonemann, Peter H., and Robert M. Carroll. 1970. Fitting One Matrix to Another under Choice of a Similarity Transformation and a Rigid Motion. *Psychometrika*, 35:245–55.

Schneider, David, J., Albert H. Hastorf, and Phoebe C. Ellsworth. 1979. *Person Perception*, 2d ed. Reading, MA: Addison-Wesley.

Shabad, Goldie, and Kristi Andersen. 1979. Candidate Evaluations by Men and Women. *Public Opinion Quarterly*, 43:19–35.

Stokes, Donald E. 1966. Some Dynamic Elements of Contests for the Presidency. *American Political Science Review*, 60:19–28.

Taylor, Shelley E., and Jennifer Crocker. 1981. Schematic Bases of Social Information Processing. In E. Tory Higgins, Charles A. Herman, and Mark P. Zanna, eds., *Social Cognition*. Hillsdale, NJ: Lawrence Erlbaum Associates.

Taylor, Shelley E., and Susan T. Fiske. 1978. Salience Attention and Attribution: Top of the Head Phenomena. In Leonard Berkowitz, ed., *Advances in Experimental Social Psychology*, vol. 11. New York: Academic Press.

Tesser, Abraham. 1978. Self-Generated Attitude Change. In Leonard Berkowitz, ed., *Advances in Experimental Social Psychology*, vol. 11. New York: Academic Press.

Wattenberg, Martin P. 1984. *The Decline of American Political Parties, 1952–1980*. Cambridge, MA: Harvard University Press.

Weisberg, Herbert F., and Jerrold G. Rusk. 1970. Dimensions of Candidate Evaluations. *American Political Science Review*, 64:1167–85.

Zajonc, Robert B. 1980. Feeling and Thinking: Preferences Need No Inferences. *American Psychologist*, 39:151–75.

Arthur H. Miller is Professor of Political Science, University of Iowa, Iowa City, IA 52240.

Martin P. Wattenberg is Assistant Professor, School of Social Sciences, University of California—Irvine, Irvine, CA 92717.

Oksana Malanchuk is a Research Analyst with Frank N. Magid Associates, Marion, IA 52302.

APPENDIX B

DO BLACK JUDGES MAKE A DIFFERENCE?*

SUSAN WELCH
University of Nebraska—Lincoln

MICHAEL COMBS
Louisiana State University

JOHN GRUHL
University of Nebraska—Lincoln

Previous examinations of the sentencing behavior of black and white trial judges failed to take into account the prior record of the

*The authors acknowledge with thanks the cooperation of court officials in Metro City. Susan Welch also wishes to acknowledge the support of the National Institute of Justice, Grant No. 84-IJ-CX-0035, which partially funded the preparation and analysis of this data set.

SOURCE: Reprinted with permission of *The American Journal of Political Science* 32:1, February 1988.

defendant; did not examine the decision to incarcerate, perhaps the most important decision in sentencing a felony defendant; and omitted controls for other salient characteristics of the judge. Analysis of the decisions to incarcerate made by black and white trial judges in a large northeastern community reveal that black judges are more even-handed in their treatment of black and white defendants than are white judges, who tend to treat white defendants somewhat more leniently. In overall sentence severity, where little racial discrimination has been found, white judges treat black and white defendants equally severely, while black judges treat black defendants somewhat more leniently than white defendants. While the impact of black judges is, therefore, somewhat mixed, in the crucial decision to incarcerate, having more black judges increases equality of treatment.

In 1852, when he was appointed to Boston's magistrate court, Robert Morris became the nation's first black judge. However, over the next century fewer than two dozen blacks presided over state or federal courts (Smith, 1983). The civil rights movement championed the representation of blacks on the bench, and beginning in the late 1960s, more were appointed and elected at all levels of government. For example, President Carter appointed 28 blacks to federal district courts and an additional nine to federal appellate courts. But have black judges made a difference in the kind of justice meted out in our nation's courts?

To answer that question, one must consider the kinds of differences black judges could make. Civil rights advocates fought for more black judges, presumably because they believed that black judges would provide both symbolic and substantive representation for black people and thus contribute to a more equitable society (see Pitkin, 1967, and Mosher, 1968, for a discussion of representation). By symbolic representation, we mean simply that blacks can look to the courts and see members of their own race in positions of influence and decision-making authority. About one-third of black judges believe that providing symbolic pride, inspiration, and status for blacks is an important function of their service on the bench (Smith, 1983). Advocates of greater minority representation on the bench also believed they would provide greater substantive representation; that is, that blacks on the bench would act in a manner to advance the best interest of blacks, reducing vestiges of racism that still remained in the legal system (Crockett, 1970). Almost 40 percent of black judges believe that this kind of substantive representation is an important function of their being judges (Smith, 1983).

Our study will focus on one aspect of substantive representation. We address the degree to which black judges act in a manner different from white judges in sentencing criminal defendants, an important aspect of trial court judge behavior.

Literature Review

During the past fifteen years there have been several studies on the attitudes, background, and recruitment of black judges (Cook, 1971; Uhlman, 1977; Smith, 1983; Slotnick, 1984), but there has been little research on their behavior (Uhlman, 1978; Gottschall, 1983; Walker and Barrow, 1985). Yet, there are reasons to expect black judges to behave differently than white judges do. Black judges tend to identify themselves as liberal rather than conservative (Smith, 1983), reflecting the general tendency of blacks to take more liberal positions than whites take on domestic and foreign issues (Seltzer and Smith, 1985; Welch and Combs, 1983). Their more liberal attitudes might make black judges more sympathetic to criminal defendants than white judges are, since liberal views are associated with support for the underdog and the poor, which defendants disproportionately are. Moreover, their background might make them especially sympathetic to black defendants (Schuman, 1971; Smith, 1983).

We do not make the assumption that the black community expects black judges to find black criminal defendants "not guilty." After all, blacks themselves are the predominant victims of black criminals. However, members of the black community are concerned whether black defendants will receive fair treatment in the court system. This concern is at least partially justified by studies of sentences received by black defendants that often find at least some discrimination against these defendants (for reviews see Kleck, 1981; Spohn, Gruhl, and Welch, 1981–82; Hagan and Bumiller, 1983). If black judges do not discriminate against black defendants, they are not "letting them off," but merely seeing to it that these defendants do not get harsher treatment than they deserve, that is, harsher treatment than white defendants get in comparable cases.

If black judges are responsive to the black community, then, one would expect them to be less likely to exhibit discrimination against black defendants by sentencing them as harshly. However, the few studies of the behavior of black judges are inconclusive. Uhlman (1978) analyzed cases from "Metro City" from 1968 to 1974 and found that both black and white judges convicted black defendants more readily and sentenced them more harshly than they did white defendants. Compared to white judges, black judges were somewhat less likely to convict black defendants as readily or sentence them as harshly, but the difference between black and white judges were small.

Walker and Barrow (1985) examined federal district court judges appointed by President Carter. They found no significant differences between black and white judges in criminal cases or in four other categories of cases, including one encompassing civil rights issues (race discrimination, school desegregation, employment rights, and police brutality). On the other hand, Gottschall (1983) examined federal appellate court judges appointed by Carter and found a dramatic difference between black and white judges in criminal defendants' and prisoners' rights cases. Black judges voted to support these rights to a substantially greater extent. Yet there were no significant differences between the judges in race or sex discrimination cases.

Of these studies, Uhlman's (1978) is most relevant to the treatment of criminal defendants because it focuses on state courts, through which the vast majority of criminal defendants are processed. Though valuable as a first step, Uhlman's study has three shortcomings which could affect its findings. It failed to control for the defendant's prior criminal record. There is nearly unanimous agreement that this record is important in understanding the defendant's sentence. Researchers have concluded that this record generally is the most important variable in explaining the decision to sentence the defendant to prison rather than to probation and often is the second most important variable, after the offense, in explaining the decision to sentence the defendant to prison for a particular length of time (for a review, see Spohn, Gruhl, and Welch, 1981–82).

Uhlman's study also failed to divide the sentence decision into two separate decisions: the decision to incarcerate or not and the length of incarceration. His study used a 93-point scale that encompassed both. Though a less obvious shortcoming than omission of prior criminal record, this approach can mask discrimination (Nagel, 1969). These are separate decisions based on somewhat different criteria. Some previous work has found discrimination against black defendants more likely in the decision to incarcerate than in the overall sentence (Spohn, Gruhl, and Welch, 1981–82).

A third potential problem is that Uhlman did not look at other characteristics of the judge that might affect decision making. We should not assume that race is the only potential predictor of judicial decision making. Factors such as previous prosecutorial experience, time on the bench, and sex might also affect how a judge treats defendants.

Given the increased number of black judges, the likelihood that their number will continue to increase, and the methodological problems of the best attempt to examine the sentencing behavior of black trial court judges, we believe that a further examination of such behavior is needed. Our study also analyzes cases from "Metro City" in an effort to compare the sentencing of black and white judges. It surmounts previous methodological difficulties by using numerous controls, including one for the prior record, and by dividing the sentence decision into two separate decisions.

Data and Methods

Our study is based on a sample of 3,418 male defendants convicted of a felony between 1968 and 1979 in a large northeastern city, which we call Metro City.[1] For each case, we have information about the defendant and his crime, his attorney, and the judge who sentenced the defendant. Of particular interest, of course, is the race of the judge.

---

[1]In exchange for access to computerized data, we had to guarantee anonymity for the city. Our case base is smaller than that used in previous studies of Metro City because in order to include prior criminal record we had to hand code that information from a different file.

But we also have data on the judge's sex, length of time on the bench, and whether or not the judge has prior prosecutorial experience.[2]

Our data included decisions made by 10 black judges and 130 white ones. While the number of black judges is small, it is comparable with the number of judges examined in previous studies (cf. Gruhl, Welch, and Spohn, 1981; Gibson, 1978).[3]

Variables

Two dependent variables will be examined. One is a dichotomous variable indicating whether (= 1) or not (= 0) the convicted defendant was sentenced to prison. The other is a sentence severity scale that ranges from 0 (suspended sentence) to 93 (life imprisonment) and includes various categories of fines, probation, and prison terms. This scale has been used before (cf. Cook, 1973; Uhlman, 1977, 1978; Spohn, Gruhl, and Welch, 1981–82; Welch, Gruhl, and Spohn, 1984) and appears to be a good measure of the range of sentencing severity.

We used a three-step procedure to assess the impact of the judge's race on each of the two measures of sentencing severity. First, we examined the bivariate relationship between the judge's race and the dependent variable. Then, we controlled for those legal and extralegal factors about the defendant and his case that are good predictors of sentencing. These factors included the most serious charge on which the defendant was convicted. This measure was a set of dummy variables for murder, manslaughter, robbery, assault, rape, minor assault, burglary, auto theft, embezzlement, stolen property, forgery, driving while intoxicated, sex offenses other than rape, and drug offenses. Murder was the omitted category.

---

[2]From our original file of defendants in Metro City between 1968 and 1979, we eliminated women, defendants not convicted, and defendants for which we have no information about the background of the judge.

[3]Using the sentencing decision as the unit of analysis automatically weights the impact of judges making only a few decisions relative to those making many. No one judge dominated the decision making. In the black sample, seven judges heard more than 50 cases each; in the white sample more than 20 did so. No black judge decided more than 150 cases, and no white judge more than 165 cases.

We also controlled for the defendant's prior record by assessing whether or not the defendant had a record of at least one prison sentence of more than one year. Previous work has shown that a prior record of a prison term is the best predictor of whether a defendant will receive a prison term (Sutton, 1978, p. 49; Harries, 1978, pp. 103–04; Vera Foundation, 1977, p. 136) and the second-best predictor after the offense in predicting sentence severity (Tiffany, Avichai, and Peters, 1975, pp. 378–79; Burke and Turk, 1975, p. 326; Sutton, 1978, p. 49; Neubauer, 1979, pp. 397–98). Having had a prison term of more than a year is a much better predictor of sentencing than arrest or conviction record (Welch, Gruhl, and Spohn, 1984; Spohn and Welch, 1986).

We also took into account two extralegal factors sometimes found to be important in predicting the sentence. These included whether (= 1) or not (= 0) the defendant has a public defender and whether (= 1) or not (= 0) the defendant entered a guilty plea.

In the third step of the analysis, after examining the bivariate relationship between the judge's race and sentencing, then adding the controls for the important legal and extralegal factors that determine sentencing, we entered three characteristics of the judges themselves. These included the gender of the judge. While few differences appear between the sentencing patterns of male and female judges, some differences in sentencing of male and female defendants have been found (Gruhl, Welch, and Spohn, 1981). It is certainly possible that male and female judges behave differently toward defendants of different races. If so, it would be useful to control for the sex of the judge in examining interracial patterns of sentencing.

We also controlled for the judge's time on the bench. One might argue that increased time on the bench could harden the judge and thereby increase the severity of his or her sentences. Indeed, in our data there was a significant bivariate relationship between time on the bench and severity of sentence. Of course, this could also be a cohort effect reflecting the eras when the judges of differing seniorities were appointed.

The final control was the judge's prior prosecutorial experience. Common wisdom suggests, even though there is little systematic evidence to prove it, that those with prosecutorial experience may be more likely to sentence severely.

Procedures

Two different procedures were mandated by the difference in the nature of the dependent variables. For the sentence severity score, ordinary least squares regression, probably the most common multivariate technique used by social scientists, was used. However, the dichotomous variable measuring whether or not the defendant was sentenced to prison is considered by many unsuitable for regression because of its noncontinuous nature. Thus, we used probit analysis. Probit analysis yields maximum likelihood estimates (MLEs). These coefficients represent the change in the cumulative normal probability resulting from a one-unit change in the independent variable. The MLEs divided by their standard errors are similar to a z distribution, which allows tests for their significance (see Fiorina, 1981, Appendix A; Aldrich and Cnudde, 1975; McKelvey and Zavoina, 1975).

Our three-stage analysis procedure, examining differences between black and white judges without controls, with controls for the defendant and his case, then finally with controls for other characteristics of the judges themselves, has already been outlined. Because we believed that there might be different patterns of sentencing for judges when they faced defendants of their own race, we examined white and black defendants separately as well as together.

Findings

Sentencing to Prison

Our expectations, based on past work, were that black judges would tend to be somewhat less severe in their sentencing patterns than white judges. These expectations were confounded in our data. Table 1 displays the findings.

Looking first at the findings for all defendants, we find that black judges are *more* severe than white judges. This finding obtains even when we control for the nature of the crime, the prior record of the defendant, and the extralegal factors of the guilty plea and type of

TABLE 1   THE IMPACT OF A JUDGE'S RACE ON SENTENCE
SEVERITY AND THE DECISION TO INCARCERATE

	Decision to Incarcerate		Sentence Severity		
	MLE	MLE/SE	b	beta	t
All Defendants					
No controls	.10	2.10*	−.48	−.01	−.67
Controls for defendant and crime	.14	2.17*	−.91	−.02	−1.60
Controls for judge, defendant, and crime	.11	1.67	−1.22	−.03	−2.14*
White Defendants					
No controls	.11	.92	.27	.01	.20
Controls for defendant and crime	.35	2.19*	1.40	.04	1.31
Controls for judge, defendant, and crime	.35	2.18*	1.39	.04	1.30
Black Defendants					
No controls	.10	1.72	−.80	−.02	−.96
Controls for defendant and crime	.09	1.24	−1.59	−.04	−2.40*
Controls for judge, defendant, and crime	.06	.78	−2.00	−.05	−2.99*

CODING: Black judges = 1, white judges = 0. Controls for defendant and crime include the severity of the crime, whether the defendant pled guilty, the defendant's prior record, and whether or not he had a public defender. Additional controls for judicial characteristics include the judge's prosecutorial experience, sex, and years on the bench. N = 3,418 for all defendants, 763 for white defendants, and 2,655 for black defendants.
* = significant at .05.

attorney. While the MLE coefficients do not allow an easy translation into percent changes in the dependent variable, the coefficients are strongly significant. When controls for the judge's sex, prosecutorial experience, and time on the bench are added, however, the difference is no longer significant.[4]

Examining prison sentences for white and black defendants sepa-

---

[4]Since the relationship is in the opposite direction hypothesized, a two-tailed test of significance seemed the most appropriate. By a one-tailed test, this difference is significant.

rately, we find an interesting pattern. In the treatment of *black* defendants, the differences between white and black judges are not significant. However, black judges are significantly more likely to sentence *white* defendants to prison than are white judges. The pattern, while not apparent at the bivariate level, emerges quite strongly when the nature of the crime, prior record, and extralegal factors of the case are controlled, and it maintains a significant relationship even when the other characteristics of the judges are also controlled.

This raises the question of whether black judges are exceptionally severe with white defendants and, for that reason, sentence them more harshly than do white judges, or whether white judges tend to sentence white defendants more leniently than they do blacks. Overall, in Metro City, there is some evidence that black defendants are sentenced to prison more than white defendants (Spohn, Gruhl, and Welch, 1981–1982). This suggests that perhaps white judges treat white defendants somewhat more leniently than black defendants. In fact, we found that white judges *are* more likely to send black defendants to prison than they are white defendants (MLE/SE = 1.63, just short of significance at the .05 level), controlling for legal and extralegal factors and other judge's characteristics. However, black judges tend to sentence black and white defendants to prison at about the same rate (MLE/SE = −.31). Thus, the fairest conclusion is that the reason black judges are more likely than white judges to send white defendants to prison is that black judges tend to treat black and white defendants alike, while white judges are more severe with black, compared with white, defendants.

Sentencing Severity

Findings for overall sentence severity differ from those concerning incarceration. Black judges give somewhat lighter sentences overall than white judges. Without controls, these differences are far from significant, but when legal and extralegal factors are controlled, these differences approach significance.[5] And, when other characteristics of

[5]Here we used a one-tailed test, since the differences are in the predicted direction. For a one-tailed test, a *t*-value of 1.645 is significant at the .05 level.

judges are controlled, the sentences of black judges are significantly less severe than those of white judges. However, these differences are substantively modest, amounting to a 1.22 difference on the 93-point scale. The difference between the coefficients when only legal and extralegal factors are controlled, compared with when the judge's characteristics are added, is a result of the fairly strong impact of time on the bench ($t = 2.32$) and prosecutorial experience ($t = -3.14$) on sentence severity. Since black judges have been on the bench slightly longer than the white judges in our sample ($r = .10$) and since they are very slightly less likely to have prosecutorial experience ($r = -.05$), controlling these factors isolates the impact of the judge's race.

That black judges sentence more defendants to prison means that they are more likely to send less serious offenders to prison than white judges do. Thus, for these defendants they give relatively shorter terms.

Examining sentence severity for black and white defendants separately, we find that black judges may give white defendants somewhat *more severe* sentences than do white judges, but the differences are far from significant. But for black defendants, black judges give *lighter sentences* than do white judges. The differences are highly significant after legal and extralegal factors have been controlled and increase their significance when the characteristics of the judge are controlled.

Again, we must ask whether these differences indicate that the black judges treat black defendants more leniently than they do whites or whether white judges treat black defendants more severely than they do whites. In examining the severity of the sentences given black and white defendants, we find that white judges may sentence blacks somewhat more severely than they do whites, but the difference is far from significant ($t = .87$, $b = .63$). Black judges sentence blacks somewhat less severely than they do whites ($t = 1.52$, $b = -1.82$), although this difference is only significant at the .10 level. Nonetheless, it tentatively appears that black judges may slightly favor defendants of their own race when determining the overall harshness of the sentence, while white judges probably do not do so. However, in the decision about incarceration, black judges appear evenhanded, while white judges are less likely to send whites than blacks to prison.

Conclusions

Racial differences in judicial sentencing behavior are only beginning to be explored. Our study goes beyond previous analyses of racial differences in the behavior of trial judges in three ways. We control for prior criminal record; we divide the sentence decision into two separate components, examining both overall sentence severity and whether or not a defendant is incarcerated. We also control for other characteristics of the judge that might help explain sentencing. We find significant differences, though modest in magnitude, in sentencing by black and white judges. Black judges are more likely than white judges to sentence white defendants to prison and to give less severe sentences to black defendants.

Thus, black judges provide more than symbolic representation. At least those in Metro City also provide substantive representation for black defendants and presumably the black community. To the extent they equalize the criminal justice system's treatment of black and white defendants, as they seem to for the crucial decision to incarcerate, they thwart discrimination against black defendants. In fact, the quality of justice received by both black and white defendants may be improved. Moreover, black judges may see this simply as part of the larger challenge of reducing discrimination against black persons in general.

There is an interesting parallel between these findings and those concerning women judges. Here we found that black judges tend to treat black and white defendants more equally than do white judges. Elsewhere, it has been found that women judges tend to treat men and women defendants more equally than do male judges (Gruhl, Welch, and Spohn, 1981). Thus, having a more representative judiciary may have some small, but visible, effects on increasing equality of treatment of criminal defendants.

That black judges behave differently from white judges is significant, given the factors that might lead them to behave similarly. Black judges experience the socialization process in law school and the legal profession that encourages lawyers and judges to adhere to the prevailing laws and precedents. Black judges in Metro City apparently were selected in the manner similar to white judges (Uhlman, 1977, 1979). Moreover, once on the bench, judges do not exercise discretion freely even in sentencing. The power of individual judges is circumscribed by the role of "court work groups": the prosecutors, defense attorneys, and judges who work together day after day to process their caseload (Eisenstein and Jacob, 1977). The participants in the work groups develop shared norms about the seriousness of various cases and the appropriateness of various punishments. These norms constrain individual judges. Gottschall (1983), who found no differences between black and white federal appellate court judges in race discrimination cases, also speculated that black judges might be circumspect in issues so salient to their own lives that they would bend over backward to try to appear unbiased.

Yet, there are reasons why black and white judges might behave slightly differently. Gottschall did find differences in criminal defendants' and prisoners' rights cases, where the connection between the judges' race and their decisions was less direct and apparent than in discrimination cases. Similarly, Metro City trial court judges might find the connection between their race and their sentence decisions indirect enough that they feel free to reflect their views. In addition, state trial court judges and their decisions are far less visible than federal appellate court judges and their decisions. There are many state trial court judges deciding many cases, usually involving routine law, while there are comparatively few federal appellate court judges deciding few cases, often involving controversial law. Even if trial judges were more visible, providing evenhanded treatment of black and white defendants would presumably be approved by the society at large; at least in the rhetoric of American politics, discrimination is not endorsed.

These findings about judges in one city, of course, might not be reflective of judicial behavior in other cities. Given the likelihood of increasing numbers of black judges, researchers will be able to conduct similar research in other jurisdictions in the future. And, as more black judges hear more cases, and as newer generations of white judges assume the trial court bench, perhaps existing racial discrimination in sentencing will disappear.

Appendix B

References

Aldrich, John, and Charles Cnudde. 1975. Probing the bounds of conventional wisdom: A comparison of regression, probit, and discriminant analyses. *American Journal of Political Science*, 19:571–608.

Burke, Peter J., and Austin T. Turk. 1975. Factors affecting postarrest decisions: A model for analysis. *Social Problems*, 22:313–32.

Cook, Beverly B. 1971. Black representation in the Third Branch. *Black Law Journal*, 1:260–79.

———. 1973. Sentencing behavior of federal judges: Draft cases, 1972. *University of Cincinnati Law Review*, 42:597–633.

Crockett, George W., Jr. 1970. Racism in the courts. *Journal of Public Law*, 20:685–88.

Eisenstein, James, and Herbert Jacob. 1977. *Felony justice: An organizational analysis*. Boston: Little, Brown.

Fiorina, Morris. 1981. *Retrospective voting in American national elections*. New Haven: Yale University Press.

Gibson, James. 1978. Race as a determinant of criminal sentence: A methodological critique and a case study. *Law and Society Review*, 12:455–78.

Gottschall, Jon. 1983. Carter's judicial appointments: The influence of affirmative action and merit selection on voting on the U.S. Court of Appeals. *Judicature*, 67.10:165–73.

Gruhl, John, Susan Welch, and Cassia Spohn. 1981. Women as policy makers: The case of trial judges. *American Journal of Political Science*, 25:308–22.

Hagan, John, and Kristin Bumiller. 1983. Making sense of sentencing: A review and critique of sentencing research. In A. Bernstein, J. Cohen, S. Martin, and M. Tonry, eds., *Research on sentencing*, vol. 2. Washington, DC: National Academy Press.

Harries, K. D. 1978. *The geography of laws and justice*. New York: Praeger.

Kleck, Gary. 1981. Racial discrimination in criminal sentencing. *American Sociological Review*, 46:783–805.

McKelvey, Richard, and William Zavoina. 1975. A statistical model for the analysis of ordinal level variables. *Journal of Mathematical Sociology*, 11:103–20.

Mosher, Frederick, 1968. *Democracy and the public service*. New York: Oxford University Press.

Nagel, Stuart. 1969. *The legal process from a behavioral perspective*. Homewood, IL: Dorsey.

Neubauer, David W. 1979. *America's courts and the criminal justice system*. North Scituate, MA: Duxbury.

Pitkin, Hanna. 1967. *The concept of representation*. Berkeley: University of California Press.

Schuman, Jerome. 1970/71. A black lawyers study. *Howard Law Journal*, 16:256–62.

Seltzer, Richard, and Robert Smith. 1985. Race and ideology. *Phylon*, 46:98–105.

Slotnick, Elliot. 1984. The paths to the federal bench: Gender, race, and judicial recruitment variation. *Judicature*, 67.10:371–88.

Smith, Michael David. 1983. *Race versus the robe: The dilemma of black judges*. New York: National University Publications.

Spohn, Cassia, John Gruhl, and Susan Welch. 1981–82. The effect of race on sentencing: A reexamination of an unsettled question. *Law and Society Review*, 16:72–88.

Spohn, Cassia, and Susan Welch. 1986. The effect of the impact of prior record in judge's sentencing decisions. *Justice Quarterly*, 3:389–408.

Sutton, L. Paul. 1978. *Variations in federal criminal sentences: A statistical assesssment at the national level*. Albany, NY: Criminal Justice Research Center.

Tiffany, Lawrence P., Yakov Avichai, and Geoffrey W. Peters. 1975. A statistical analysis of sentencing and federal courts: Defendants convicted after trial, 1967–1968. *Journal of Legal Studies*, 4:369–90.

Uhlman, Thomas, 1977. Race, recruitment, and representation: Background differences between black and white trial court judges. *Western Political Quarterly*, 31:457–70.

———. 1978. Black elite decision making: The cases of trial judges. *American Journal of Political Science*, 22:884–95.

———. 1979. *Racial justice*. Lexington, MA: Lexington Books.

Vera Foundation. 1977. *Felony arrests: Their prosecution and disposition in New York City's courts*. New York: Longman.

Walker, Thomas G., and Deborah J. Barrow. 1985. The diversification of the federal bench: Policy and process ramifications. *Journal of Politics*, 47:596–616.

Welch, Susan, and Michael W. Combs. 1983. Interracial differences in opinions on public issues in the 1970's. *Western Journal of Black Studies*, 7:136–41.

Welch, Susan, John Gruhl, and Cassia Spohn. 1984. Sentencing: The influence of alternative measures of prior record. *Criminology*, 22:215–28.

INDEX

Action research. *See* Participatory action research
Actuality, 138–39
Alternative variables, 76
Antecedent variables, 76–77
Applied research, 153
Aristotle, 23
Asherson, Samuel, 140n
Association, 108–9
  and descriptive statistics, 108
  Goodman-Kruskal's gamma, 114–15
  nominal measurement, 111–13
  variables in, 108
  See also Correlation
Athanasiou, Robert, 85n

Ball, Terence, 147n
Bean, Clive, 61n
Becker, Howard S., 140n
Beta coefficient, 123–24
Bias
  in sample, 105
  survey data, 59–60
Bibliography, 54–55
Bivariate regression, 119–20, 127
  definition of, 130
  example of, 119–20
  purpose of, 119
Blumer, Herbert, 140n
Bobo, Lawrence, 40, 43n

Bohrnstedt, G.W., 113
Browning, Rufus, 41n

Carmines, Edward G., 30n
Causal relationships, 82–84
  and hypothesis formation, 83–84
  origin of, 118
  proof requirements in, 82–83
Chass, Murray, 120
Chi-square, 112–13
Chun, Ki-Taek, 85n
Clausen, Aage, 157n
Coefficient of determination, 124
Coles, Robert, 157n
Combs, Michael, 126, 128, 129, 179
Computers, and measurement, 131
Concepts, 18–20
  and deduction, 71–72
  nature of, 18–20
  operationalizing of, 52–54
  and science, 20–21
  variables as, 21–23
Conformity, 148–49
  factors related to, 148–49
Connolly, William, 156n
Contingency coefficient in, 111–13
  computation of, 112–13
Continuous quantification, 27–28
Control, and multiple regression, 126–27

195

Kenneth Hoover (Ph.D., University of Wisconsin-Madison) is Chair and Professor of Political Science at Western Washington University. His recent books include *Ideology and Political Life*, second edition (Wadsworth, 1994) and (with Raymond Plant) *Conservatism and Capitalism in Britain and the United States* (Routledge, 1989).

Todd Donovan (Ph.D., University of California, Riverside) is Professor of Political Science at Western Washington University. His recent publications include articles in *Studies in Community Sociology* (JAI Press, 1994) and *Electoral Strategies and Political Marketing* (Macmillan, 1992).